DACOTAH TERRITORY
A 10 YEAR ANTHOLOGY

Edited by Mark Vinz and Grayce Ray

North Dakota Institute for Regional Studies, Fargo, 1982

Cover: photograph from *Dacotah Territory* 5, by Linda Hanson
Logo designed by Paul Wong

Typesetting by Alpha Typesetters
Printing by Richtman's-Midwest

ISBN 0-911042-26-1
© North Dakota Institute for Regional Studies, Fargo 1982

Table of Contents

A Note on the Selection and Arrangement of Poems

All of the poems in this collection were originally published in *Dacotah Territory* Magazine; we decided against selecting any poems we reprinted from other magazines or books, and also against selecting either prose poems or translations. Finally, we decided to present the poems alphabetically, by author. An appendix listing the poems in the order they originally appeared (by issue) may be found at the end of this book.

Looking Back on Ten Years of *Dacotah Territory*

Mark Vinz

Dacotah Territory has just completed its tenth year of publication, a pretty good record for a little magazine from America's hinterlands: 17 issues, 15 books and chapbooks of poetry, and huge amounts of time, patience, and dreaming. While we've been able to watch the magazine grow from a small and simple and mostly regional publication to a much larger and nationally distributed one, we've still tried to maintain ties to those same ideals with which we began. That makes it even more difficult to end the magazine. But while I've certainly had a lot of encouragement to keep it going under just about *any* circumstances, there comes a time when the energies simply run out, as do the time and money. Several years ago I began to think about the best ways to end *Dacotah Territory*, and my hope for a final, "retrospective" anthology is now being fulfilled thanks to the North Dakota State University Institute for Regional Studies. As has been the history of the magazine, there are always good people there just when you need them.

So, what I'll try to do in the next paragraphs is provide some kind of brief history of the magazine—what motivated it, what sustained it, and how it has evolved over 10 years. That too is a very difficult thing to do, and as I sit here trying to sort it all out, trying to assess the impact it has made on me and those around me, I'm struck again by the whole phenomenon of small press publishing in this country—its contribution to the strength and vitality of American Letters and to the relationships among a large number of people. To be sure, the decade of the 70's has been a very exciting time to be involved with small press: one has only to look at the steady growth of *The International Directory of Little Magazines and Small Presses*, to listen to the continuing dialogue on the decentralization of American publishing, to realize that small press ("noncommercial press" is probably a better term) is more than just the breeding and proving ground for American writers; indeed, it's the place we can find much of the best poetry and fiction today.

What makes all this even more amazing is the force behind most small presses and literary magazines. It certainly isn't monetary profit, for the most of us make little or nothing from our enterprises. And it's a lot more than either ego-building or the "message" of any particular school or philosophy. Tom Montag, for several years editor of *Margins: A Review of Little Mags and Small Press Books* (and a man who probably knows as much about small press as just about anyone in this country), puts it this way: "Small press exists for the sake of literature, is not bound by the necessity to produce a saleable commodity or make a profit, is free to disregard current standards of taste and excellence; it can set its own standards and can change them as they become worn." Many people find themselves using the term "labor of love," and even if that's a cliche, perhaps it comes the closest to explaining our commitment. But it doesn't begin to explain the impact small press publishing can make on one's life. Indeed, those of us who have worked with magazines and presses have seen our lives drastically changed in the past decade.

When I came to teach at Moorhead State University in northwestern Minnesota in 1968, I had no idea what I would be involved with in just a few years. Fresh from graduate school at the Universities of Kansas and New Mexico, I was a teacher of English who occasionally wrote poems; soon I was to be a magazine editor in contact with hundreds of writers from all over the country, exchanging publications with dozens of magazines and presses, and participating in a tremendously exciting experiment in small press distribution that would eventually lead to such things as a bookbus touring the Upper Midwest and my inclusion on a panel on American publishing at the Library of Congress. The history of *Dacotah Territory* has been a history of what I could never have predicted: how a place like Moorhead, Minnesota and its sister city of Fargo, North Dakota could ever produce a flourishing literary community (and my, how those

1

first winters *here were cold*); how I could become caught up in a study of the regional impulse in general and of my own roots (Minnesota and North Dakota) in particular; how I would become possessed by poetry, my own and that of many others; how even up here on the "Far Edge" I would meet so many fine people—writers and dreamers and sharers.

The history of *Dacotah Territory*—like that of any magazine—has been primarily a history of individuals, and acknowledging the aid and support of a number of them seems the only proper place to begin this retrospective: poets Thomas McGrath, Gene Frumkin, and Robert Bly, who provided much of the inspiration and encouragement at the outset; Moorhead State University president Roland Dille and MSU printer Tom Rickart, who have seen to it that the magazine, since 1973, got printed; associate editor Grayce Ray, who has provided invaluable help and insight since our fourth issue, and the others who have been associate editors at one time or another: Dale Jacobson, Michael Moos, Tim Hagen, and Robert Waldridge; graphic designer Paul Wong, who established our format and logo, Jay Holmen, who acted as business manager during our most difficult years; and Larry Peterson, our first distributor; poet James L. White, who guest edited our two Native American poetry collections, and who has remained a trusted friend and counsel, as have George Roberts, Robert Schuler, and Steve Ward, especially in helping with this final manuscript; Joseph Richardson, whose Plains Distribution Service has been of tremendous importance to *DT* and dozens of other magazines and presses, as has the work in distribution of David Wilk (Truck Distribution) and Jim Sitter (Bookslinger); my wife, Betsy, typist and proofreader, who has supported and encouraged in so many ways. The list could go on—writers, editors, friends—but one man in particular, Leonard Randolph, needs special mention here. No one in the last ten years has been as dedicated to the care and survival of American small presses as Len Randolph, Literature Program Director for the National Endowment for the Arts, 1970-78; his presence as an advocate for small press publishing, funding, and distribution, as a visionary and innovator, has been a major contribution to American literature. Without his support, we simply couldn't have done very much—and many other editors can no doubt make the same statement.

It is in a spirit of appreciation and gratitude, then, that this final *Dacotah Territory* collection is dedicated to all those who have helped so much, but especially to Len Randolph, Tom McGrath, Jim White, and Joe Richardson. These are the names which come up so very often in *Dacotah Territory's* 10 years.

Dacotah Territory magazine began with an idea of a healthy and diversified regionalism, and it was that spirit that provided the direct impetus for the first part of its history. Our original statement of intent appeared on the inside front cover of *Dacotah Territory* number 1, 1971:

> Dacotah Territory...not to be confused with the Dakotas or the U.S. government's territorial boundaries of 1861...is what we now call the Great Plains—the lands originally inhabited by the Dacotah or Sioux nation of tribes, stretching from the Great Lakes and the Mississippi to the Rockies, and from Canada southward to the Oklahoma Territories and beyond. The word Dacotah means "allies." To unfriendly tribes it means "enemies."

That statement was inspired in part by Stephen Mooney's *Tennessee Poetry Journal* and by George Hitchcock's *Kayak*. What we wanted was a title, like Hitchcock's, that suggested just what we were all about (though a kayak is a vessel for individuals while we sensed an almost tribal solidarity among writers on the Plains), and at the same time we believed strongly that our particular sense of the regional must not be insular, as did Mooney: "to affirm the sense of place as a source for poetry; to bring those on the outside in, to send those on the inside out." In short, while we had begun to discover that there was a literary flowering all around us in the Upper Midwest, this was also happening across the country, nurtured by the decentralizing power of the small press movement itself. We learned very early that, as Donald Davidson had charted so many years before in his *Attack on Leviathan*, the real health of American writing seemed to be in regions, and often in that which sought to resist the so-called "national" culture and its media blitzes from New York and the West Coast. That kind of thinking was particularly heartening to Midwesterners, especially considering the long tradition of Midwestern literary expatriates, and the fact that Midwestern audiences were still well trained to take their cues from far away and thus overlook much of what was in their midst. It was that kind of dialogue that a number of Midwestern magazines in particular were becoming involved with in the late 60's and early 70's, so we had plenty of sources to draw from—most notably John Milton's *South Dakota Review*.

On the other hand, there was still the clear danger of the regional, or the part of it associated with narrow-mindedness, insulation, and boosterism. So even from the very beginnings of *Dacotah Territory* what we sought was always two-fold: to tap into the poetry of place flourishing around us, but never to be simply limited by it; to take a stand against the placelessness of American society, but not with "down-homeism," or, as Davidson had warned, with any kind of *ism*. A sense of place as we tried to define it, then, was quite different from many people's notion of regionalism, and it was that end we sought:

> We see ourselves, then, as importers and exporters, seeking the best work from both new and established writers no matter what their *place*—that unique vitality which partakes of both the local and international simultaneously.

That statement came from our first advertising flyer, and we tried to remain true to it throughout the life of the magazine.

In general terms, then, what brought about *Dacotah Territory* was a recognition of the talents and energies around us (and the scant number of publishing outlets in the Midwest), and the gradual exploration of the term "a sense of place" and its implications. A more specific catalyst was the trouble brewing on the campus of Moorhead State in 1969 and 1970, where both the undergraduate literary magazine and the student newspaper had become embroiled in censorship disputes. As a result of those times, a group of students and I began to publish a poetry broadside called *The Fat Giraffe* and it met with a very enthusiastic response. From those efforts we began to explore the notion of a larger publication, and spurred by Antony Oldknow and his Scopcraeft Press (which, based at North Dakota State University in Fargo, had already produced a poetry magazine and chapbook series), we decided to investigate offset printing and the possibilities of extending beyond the Red River Valley. The students—Dale Jacobson, Michael Moos, and Tim Hagen—helped me raise some money (donations from a number of kind people in the area), Robert Bly, Tom McGrath, and Gene Frumkin (who had been my teacher in New Mexico) contributed poems and encouraged submissions, Richard Lyons (a poet who also taught at NDSU) let us use a long interview with McGrath (published in *DT* 1 and 2), and my wife Betsy, nine months pregnant, typed the manuscript on a rented IBM at our dining room table (where we also collated and stapled it when Betsy was in the hospital). The first issue of *Dacotah Territory* (and our second daughter, Sarah) was born in January of 1971.

The fact that there were in this area noted poets like Tom McGrath and Richard Lyons also, of course, had a great deal to do with the start of the magazine. Their counsel and friendships made a lot of exciting poetry available to us from the start, but there were also a number of talented young and beginning writers here as well. One of them, David Martinson, had tried unsuccessfully to start a poetry magazine the year before (*North Forty*), so a few of the poems from his manuscript were also incorporated in *DT* 1. Those were also the days when there were many poetry readings in Fargo-Moorhead, so we were exposed to poets such as William Stafford, Galway Kinnell, Robert Hayden, and Diane Wakoski (at MSU, from the Beloit Poetry Circuit), and Denise Levertov, George Starbuck, and Anne Sexton (at NDSU). Since Robert Bly's home in Madison, Minnesota was only 130 miles away, he was a frequent visitor, and, needless to say, his zeal had an effect on us all. The range of writers in the area, the diversity of interests, ages, and experiences, had everything to do with the beginnings of *Dacotah Territory*, and we began to learn more and more about small press in general from COSMEP publications (Committee of Small Press Editors and Publishers), and from our own failures in local and regional bookstores. Indeed, the trunk of my car became a portable magazine rack, and whenever a friend left town it was likely with a few copies of the magazine in his own trunk.

To be sure, it was slow going, and our naivete brought some setbacks; it took us a full year to produce our next issue (we had planned for three a year), encouraged by submissions from William Stafford, Gene Frumkin, Don Gordon, and Marnie Walsh. Although the magazine was still very slim (as with *DT* 1, 36 pages, 300 copies), both our zeal and our conversations about poetry were growing at a steady pace.

Dacotah Territory 3, much to everyone's surprise, was ready by the summer of 1972, made up primarily of a manuscript put together by Tom McGrath for his own magazine, *Crazy Horse*, which he'd brought out sporadically for a number of years (and from a number of places). Tom had turned over his magazine to Southwest Minnesota State College, but he and the new editors soon had a number of disagreements; *Dacotah Territory* provided a means for him to publish his final issue intact. Thus, *DT* 3, as McGrath's work itself, emphasized political poetry and comment, and contained poems by such notables as Louis Simpson, Gary Snyder, W.S. Merwin, and Robert Bly—most of whose work we'd never expected to see in our small magazine. Nonetheless, the issue seemed to solidify what we had begun; our press run was up to 500 copies, and our subscription list finally broke 100 (*DT* was selling for 75ᶜ a copy, or $2.00 for a three-issue subscription). How delighted we all were to see Elizabeth Yazzetti's annotation for *Dacotah Territory* ("One of our greatest") in the Autumn 1972 issue of *New York Quarterly's* listing of "College, Literary, and 'Little' Magazines" from around the country, and how well her comments on the magazine summed up what we were all about:

> Up to now submissions have been on a more-or-less invitational basis, but the editors are now interested in seeing poetry from "the territory" (but not "regionalist poetry"), poetry with some of the elements of surrealism (the image et al), a poetry generally open to understanding, poetry with social and political commitments, poetry of ethnic minorities, particularly the American Indian.

This is indeed where we were in 1972, though a good part of that statement would stick with us for the next eight years.

What Tom McGrath's issue accomplished certainly helped to put *Dacotah Territory* on the map, so to speak, but since it was our third issue it had the added benefit of making us eligible for a grant from the Coordinating Council of Literary Magazines (CCLM). I received word that we had been awarded $1000 from CCLM that Fall, while attending a meeting in Minneapolis set up by small press advocate Dr. Marvin Suckov—a meeting to introduce some of the editors and writers from around the state to each other. What a momentous trip it turned out to be, both for me personally and for the magazine: I met Alvin Greenberg (poet, novelist, and former editor of *Minnesota Review*), Jim White (who had just come to Minnesota from the Navajo to work in the state Poets in the Schools program), and Molly LaBerge, the remarkable director of Minnesota PITS, who was soon to put together a literature panel for the Minnesota State Arts Board (upon which I was to serve). Something exciting was definitely happening within the region, and centered in the Minneapolis-St. Paul area. It was here over the next few years that I was to come in contact with dozens of writers (many of whom would appear in *DT*), wonderful bookstores (Savran's and Rusoff's in Minneapolis, and The Hungry Mind in St. Paul), incredible literary energies of all sorts. And even though I always fancied myself an emissary from the Far Edge, both I and *DT* were accepted into the center of activity in the Twin Cities.

Another major change for the magazine at this time was the appearance on the scene of Grayce Ray, a native Canadian who had come to Moorhead via Kentucky and Arkansas. Just at the time when most of the founding editors had gone on to other things, here was someone (poet, artist, bundle of crazy energy) who could really help out with the magazine. Through Grayce, we soon had a new logo and format (designed by her friend Paul Wong), to say nothing of the new literary perspective the magazine took on as her tastes and judgments worked (and sometimes clashed) with mine. The basis for our working relationship was established right away, and I think for the good of the magazine—we each fought for what we wanted, and in so doing defined for ourselves the standards we really believed in. Over the years, by the way, there has been far more agreement than disagreement, though it's also been healthy that we've jointly published work that either of us individually might not have accepted.

Ironically, our new grant money also brought new problems, the greatest of which was in securing matching funds. A group of Minnesota magazines with grants from CCLM (and organized by James Naiden, editor of *North Stone Review*) failed to get funds from foundations. When things looked very dark, I went to Moorhead State President Roland Dille for advice and suggestions; I left his office with an agreement I hadn't even dreamed of. Moorhead State would support *Dacotah Territory* by having it printed at the MSU print shop at rates much cheaper than we would have to pay a commercial printer (as long as it in no way interfered with official college printing). In return, we would cite published *at* (not *by*) Moorhead State on the title page—a relationship that was to continue for the history of the magazine. It certainly helps to have a college president who is also a former English teacher, a lover of poetry, and a writer on your side! Not many magazines can claim this kind of relationship, nor the support of a printer like Tom Rickart—for which we remain extremely grateful.

Dacotah Territory 4 was finally published during the winter of 1972-73, expanded to 64 pages and a press run of 1000. With it came an ever-widening stream of manuscripts, many from the Los Angles area (where Tom McGrath had once taught), but many more from all over Minnesota, introducing us to poets such as Stephen Dunn, Al Zolynas, and Louis Jenkins. We also began to print a few reviews.

Dacotah Territory 5, in the fall of 1973, was again guest edited by Tom McGrath, who introduced us to Richard Hugo, Trish Hampl, and Jim Moore, with more poems from Roland Flint, Robert Bly, and William Stafford (was there ever so generous and kind a poet in America?). There was also work by a flock of young writers from Moorhead who had been Tom's students and mine (I was now teaching creative writing courses too), one of whom (Bob Waldridge) had been an associate editor for *DT* 4. Linda Hanson's cover photograph of a line of cows crossing a snowy field became the one that many people would identify the magazine with, and it remains my favorite cover of all we've done.

1973 brought some other important changes, too. Jim Fawbush, a young poet from Moorhead, came to me with a chapbook manuscript, and since a friend of Grayce's (Paulette Mertes, who also did pasteup and design work for us) was taking a course in letter press printing and needed a class project, we decided that the strength of the manuscript and the fortuitous circumstances should launch a chapbook series. Even then, Grayce and I saw that the magazine was becoming less and less a product of this region, so in part the chapbooks (authors from this area) could help to restore our import/export balance. Fawbush's *Great Grandpa Nettestad Was Blind* was ready by the fall of 1973, the first of a series of 10 chapbooks published into early 1976—and soon to be funded by a $2500 grant from the NEA, applied for with the assistance of Len Randolph. Suddenly it seemed we were becoming a kind of cottage industry, and while it was exciting to see the (20-24 page) chapbooks coming off the press, it also was frustrating to see our problems with distribution multiplied. I soon found that I was spending more time with book keeping and invoicing than with reading manuscripts—my initiation into the world of small press was becoming complete.

About this time, too, we were to launch into two other new ventures which, in terms of work expended, would replace just about everything else. The first was a sampler of poems by Tom McGrath. Swallow Press had released *The Movie At the End of the World*, his new and selected poems, but only in a hard cover edition. As Swallow kept putting Tom off about the paperback (indeed, it wasn't released until 1980), he grew more and more upset that the very people he wanted to read the poems simply couldn't afford the expensive edition. So we came up with an idea: *Dacotah Territory* (under the Territorial Press imprint which had been invented for the chapbooks) would publish a 50 poem "sampler" from the larger edition, which would help Swallow by advertising the hardcover book and also help Tom and *Dacotah Territory* as well. Swallow approved of the arrangement—one of the few instances I know of where a larger, commerical press cooperated with a small, non-commercial one. Tom and I each picked 50 poems for the sampler (we agreed on over three-fourths of them and haggled over the rest), which was titled *Voices from Beyond the Wall* and went on to sell out three printings (over 1500 copies total) in the next few years.

The second new venture was *Dacotah Territory* 6, and it was also brought about by a unique relationship—this time with James L. White and the NEA Literature Program, via Len Randolph. Jim had become a very close friend, and his experience in the Native American community seemed to present some marvelous possibilities for publication. We agreed that he should edit a special issue of the magazine, a Native American issue he would assemble from his contacts all over the country. When I told Len Randolph about the project he was excited enough to suggest that the NEA buy (at cost) 2000 copies of the issue and distribute it to all the state arts agencies in the U.S. So, during the winter of 1973-74, we dedicated full efforts to the manuscript, and 4000 copies were printed—which was as staggering to our printer, Tom Rickart, as it was to us. But it was a lovely edition and it made a tremendous impact, and for the next few years I was to have a great deal of contact with other people publishing Native American collections, and to provide some aid to Ken Rosen with his *Voices of the Rainbow: Contemporary Poetry by American Indians* (Viking Press, 1975) and some editors at Harper and Row, for Duane Niatum's *Carriers of the Dream Wheel: Contemporary Native American Poetry* (also 1975). Aside from working so closely with Jim White, the greatest joy to me from *DT* 6 was the introduction to the work of such poets as Roberta Hill, Simon Ortiz, Anita Endrezze, and Joy Harjo. Two years later we were to do a second Native American collection, again edited by Jim (but as a Territorial Press book, not an issue of the magazine), titled *The First Skin Around Me: Contemporary American Tribal Poetry*, with work by some of the same fine poets but also a number of new ones. Indeed, the history of the early years of *Dacotah Territory* is a history of discovering just how many good writers there are in this country. That, of course, is related to the large number of presses publishing poetry and fiction, especially the small and non-commercial ones.

Perhaps it's time to stop my chronological reminiscences for a while and stress again the inter-relatedness of small press publishing. While American small presses are too diverse and geographically scattered to be called a "community" (as Robert Bly has suggested, the term "net-work" is more accurate), there is still a kind of mutual support system that often operates among editors—especially since we share a unique set of problems, and we understand all too well the kinds of sacrifices our "labors of love" demand. We do tend to listen to each other, to pay atten-tion to excellence and innovation when we see it, to keep a dialogue going even if sometimes it gets a bit harsh. *Dacotah Territory*, then, is typical in that it has been much influenced by other magazines and editors. Likewise, I delight in discovering the ways we have had an impact too, which is why I'm especially pleased to have Bob Schuler's essay as a part of this anthology. In many ways the most gratifying part of being an editor is the constant contact one has with one's peers—the friendships and exchanges, the shared ideas, the valuable criticism, and the simple knowledge that there are many others out there who are at least as crazy as you are.

It has seemed to many editors that the single greatest problem we've faced (and continue to face) is that of distribution, and the related area of "audience development." Not that we want small, non-commercial presses to become large and commercially viable. Most of us don't. But being an editor means also being dedicated to getting the work into the hands of the readers, and without a system of regular publication and distribution this is a staggeringly difficult task (to say nothing of the fact that most of us aren't very good as business managers).

It is in this light that most of my proudest accomplishments in small press have come from work-ing with a number of dedicated people in the establishing and maintaining of Plains Distribution Service, Inc., a non-profit literary organization for the promotion and distribution of Midwestern authors and non-commercial presses. The Plains story will have to be written fully one day; here I only have time for a few words about how it came about—which was the direct result of in-troducing *Dacotah Territory* to one man, Joe Richardson.

Joe Richardson *is* Plains Distribution—a unique individual who mixes an acute business sense with a visionary support for literature and all the arts. He's the one person who could have started Plains, the one who could put together practical funding proposals and talk to founda-tions in their own language while at the same time maintaining a populist idealism and love of small press. From the early days (1973, about the time we were putting together *DT* 6) when he managed a cooperative bookstore in Moorhead and we began a dialogue on how small presses (especially Midwestern ones) desperately needed viable means of promotion and distribution, through the gradual building of one of the largest literary organizations in the country (with an-nual budgets of over 100,000 dollars), he has given an incredible amount with very little tangible return. Some of Plains Distribution Service's accomplishments from 1975 (the year of our first NEA grant, again with the help of Len Randolph) through 1980 include: 18 booklists advertising an average of 15 small press titles per list (and each mailed to nearly 4000 individuals and institu-tions), the organization and sponsorship (Fargo, May 1976) of a national small press distribution conference (over 20 organizations attended), a bookbus which in 1977-80 traveled Minnesota, the Dakotas, Iowa, and Wisconsin (with forays into Nebraska and Michigan) completing over 200 stops at colleges, conferences, schools, libraries, arts fairs, etc. to sell books and give workshops and readings, sponsorship of over 100 poetry and fiction readings, visits to national and regional library and book sellers conventions, and a constant and continuing advocacy of Midwestern authors and presses. Like *Dacotah Territory*, Plains maintained strong ties to a region, yet always sought ways to get beyond it as well. That was also true of Plains' sponsorship (1974-78) of a magazine committee—a series of meetings of Midwestern magazine editors to discuss common problems and explore common goals, culminating in the Plains Magazine List—brochures to advertise these magazines as a group.

Even though Plains was to receive grant support from perhaps a dozen private foundations (as well as the NEA and several state arts agencies), it still couldn't survive—which is more a comment on the limited support for literature in this country than on the many people who worked for and with the organization. In that sense, the demise of Plains has much to do with the demise of *Dacotah Territory* and other magazines and presses, yet we also know that whatever vision we shared is still there and will continue in some form. There is still a clear need for distribution programs and organizations in the small press community; though a few still remain, an alarming number have folded in the past few years—mainly non-profit enterprises. And while there are still some for-profit distributors (such as Bookslinger in St. Paul), they deal primarily with retail outlets, while Plains and its counterparts have dealt directly with individuals and libraries. Something equally important here, then, and one of the principles upon which Plains (and *Dacotah Territory*) was founded, is a belief in an audience for literature. For me, the most exciting part of small press publishing and distribution is the positive reaction of people who simply hadn't been exposed to poetry—a potentially enthusiastic audience, but one that is missed or overlooked by traditional means of distribution. Finding that audience is one more reason why Plains stands as one of the most innovative experiments in recent American publishing. That's exactly the kind of energy I've been talking about all along, which reflects again the kinds of profound changes small press can make on an individual's life.

That, I'm afraid, was a much longer than intended digression, but it was also a very necessary one.

After the Native American collection of *Dacotah Territory*, and the beginnings of Plains Distribution, the summer of 1974 brought a bit of breathing space. Issue number 7 featured an interview with (and a number of poems by) Gene Frumkin, a man who (like *his* former teacher, Tom McGrath) has done a great deal to foster and nourish poetry. Fittingly, that issue also introduced our readers to two other poets and editors who have done a great deal for poetry, especially in the Midwest: John Judson and John Milton. (Ted Kooser, a third in that category, was to have work in the next issue). By the time we were finalizing the manuscript for the next issue, however, our breathing space had disappeared, and after much discussion we decided to combine issues 8 and 9 into one "catch-up" double issue. It was also our first experience with perfect binding: we forgot to have the name of the magazine printed along the spine, and the binding job was so bad that many of the copies came apart in the mail. So much for double issues.

Aside from being a problem, *Dacotah Territory* 8/9 was also a direct return to the idea of poetry and place, in the form of an interview with Tom McGrath, John Milton, and Frederick Manfred (conducted in Milton's home in Vermillion, South Dakota, and taped by Bob Waldridge, who was then a graduate student at USD). Though we were excited about reviving the "regional" dialogue, the issue did provoke some attacks—and it also provoked continuing discussions about the direction we should be taking, since we were receiving work from a wider variety of poets (region, style, age, etc.) than ever before. By that time Jay Holmen had shown up in my office—an accounting major who also loved poetry and wanted to help out on the magazine! For the next couple of years we had a fine business manager, and for the first time my problems with the *business* side of the magazine were held in check.

In the summer of 1975, Grayce edited *Dacotah Territory 10* on her own, while I became involved editing a manuscript of new and selected poems by Jim White (*The Del Rio Hotel*, published later that year by Territorial Press), and putting together the second Native American collection. One of the nicest things to happen with *DT* 10 was the work we received from Carolyn Forché—the best poems Grayce and I had seen in some time (one appeared in *DT* 10, and one appeared in *DT* 12). She was to go on to win the Yale Younger Poets award for *Gathering the Tribes* and send a letter thanking us for being among the very first editors to praise and publish her work. That's another event that can make editing a real joy, aside from giving you some faith in your editing abilities. I've signed close to 100 copyright transfers in the last few years, and it's still a special delight to see work we've originally published included in books or anthologies. Within the past few weeks I've signed two that give me particular pleasure—one for David Wojahn, this year's Yale winner, and one for Jim White, whose *Salt Ecstasies* will soon be published by Graywolf Press.

Even if issues 7, 8/9, and 10 confirmed the fact that *Dacotah Territory* was becoming both more diverse and further behind in production, the chapbook series and other books were moving along very well. In the fall of 1974 I attended a CCLM conference in Milwaukee and met and talked with a number of writers and editors; my energies and those of small press were running exceptionally high. Then, in the fall of 1975, Leonard Randolph* helped put together a national conference on the publishing of poetry and fiction, held at the Library of Congress. I was included on the Small Press and University Press panel and was inspired to see the ways my colleagues worked from a boundless kind of optimism and energy—quite the opposite of the gloom and doom stories we kept hearing from members of the large New York trade houses. The message for publishing was very clear. The big houses and magazines were constantly cutting back on creative work, dominated by their sales and marketing divisions. The ideas, the solutions, and the enthusiasm came from the small presses and little magazines, from people like Ramona Weeks and E.V. Griffith. The responses to Plains Distribution were also very heartening—the first booklist had just been published, and I brought copies with me to Washington.

If I had a glimpse of the national small press scene, literary activity in the Midwest was just as exciting. Part of this seemed to be a result of poets in the schools programs, and Minnesota had one of the largest and most successful in the country—due in direct measure to administrators like Molly LaBerge. Just as *Dacotah Territory 1* had tried to tap into some of the energies of *place*, *DT* 11 tapped into the energies of Minnesota Poets in the Schools; it was another special issue, featuring poems by writers in the program, selected by an editorial board of myself, Jim White, John Rezmerski, and Jim Moore, with an eye toward adoption in classrooms. The issue sold out its 2000 copies in short order, with fantastic responses. It also was to give us the basis for a new Territorial Press chapbook the next year: *The Blessing of Winter Rain* by George Roberts, who was one of the most active members in the Minnesota program.

Since *Dacotah Territory* 11 was another special issue, we were again far behind in our production schedule and Grayce and I approached burn-out. The frustrations of an editor are many; for editors who are also writers, there is a kind of schizophrenia too. That fall, Capra Press published a chapbook of mine, *Letters to the Poetry Editor* (illustrated by Grayce), which tried to express some of those frustrations through parody. While *Letters* had been for the most part fun to write, it was also the outgrowth of all those (sometimes conflicting) roles we editors must fulfill, for no pay or time off: proofreading, layout, design, promoting and advertising, marketing and distribution, invoicing, packing, shipping, warehousing, bookkeeping, grant writing, the list goes on. It's no wonder our patience and resources sometimes wear thin, especially when reading manuscripts amounts to less than a fourth of what most of us do!

During the next year, the crazy game of catch-up continued. *Dacotah Territory* 12 featured an interview on "The Great Mother" with Robert Bly, a stunning cover photo of a chained cigar store Indian by Dale Amundson and Charlotte Werner, and fine poems by writers as diverse as Ray Young Bear, Betsy Adams, and Dave Etter. *Dacotah Territory* 13, which was to be our fifth anniversary issue, was published nearly a year late as our *sixth* anniversary issue (Fall 1976). Both numbers pleased me as an editor, but especially 13, which remains my favorite of all 17—probably because I decided to print, for at least part of the issue, larger quantities of work by a selected few writers: Michael Dennis Browne, Stephen Dunn, Dan Jaffe, Daniel Lusk, Gene Frumkin, Tom McGrath, Roland Flint, and William Kloefkorn. Quite simply, I indulged myself with some of my favorites. What better way to celebrate an anniversary, even if it was a year late! *DT* 13 also brought an increase in price and number of pages ($1.50 and 120) and a return (for good) to perfect binding and a press run of around 900. We finally had to admit that fewer and larger issues would be the only way we could keep up with the magazine. (Oh, how librarians must love small press: constant changes in frequency, price, and format).

The new plans made it a bit easier to play catch-up but also increased the risk of becoming too scattered. Partly to offset this, our 1977 and 1978 issues (numbers 14 and 15) each centered on long prose pieces. *Dacotah Territory* 14 (Spring-Summer 1977) presented a long review essay by Jim Moore on Tom McGrath's *Letter to An Imaginary Friend*, an essay which had originally been accepted for publication by *Chicago Review* but which had been cancelled with a change of editors. *Dacotah Territory* 15 (Winter-Spring 1977-78) presented a long essay on politics in poetry by Dale Jacobson, who was then a graduate student at the University of North Dakota. Both issues were 96 pages, but as the multiple seasons and years on our title pages indicated, we were still slipping behind in production. We finally reached the point of having to admit that we could manage only one issue a year, and we needed to formalize that fact. As a result, we decided to make our future "yearly anthologies" center on a theme.

A few years before, when Jim White had settled on the title *The Del Rio Hotel* for his new and selected poems, we had talked of our love for hotels and cafes—especially the old and out-of-the-way ones in the Midwest. It didn't take much encouragement to settle on hotels and cafes as the theme for *Dacotah Territory* 16, especially since Grayce had been working on her own manuscript: *Poems from A Residential Hotel* (later published as a Bloodroot chapbook). Partly because of the visual power of our theme, and partly because I'd been working with Wayne Gudmundson, a fine young photographer from Moorhead, we also decided to include a selection of photographs (16 pages) edited by Wayne and drawing upon some of the work from the 1976 North Dakota Photo Documentary Project. Hotels and cafes are natural metaphors and settings in the work of many poets, so we soon had a huge manuscript—made up partly of poems I wanted to reprint from books and other magazines. To be sure, it was a kind of sentimental journey for all those involved, but it's one I'm very glad we made.

Dacotah Territory 16 was published in late 1979 as *Been Here Once: Hotel and Cafe Poems with Photographs*, and we began thinking about our next issue, our next theme. We kicked around several possibilities—nature poems, political poems, satires, parodies, and poems written by or for children, to name a few—but it was Joe Richardson's suggestion, "Fathers," that finally stuck. The term itself has an awesome and immediate power of association; as with hotels and cafes, we knew we'd soon be seeing many fine poems. Likewise, the women's movement had already been making a real impact on small presses, and *fathers* seemed to strike out in a new (yet at the same time familiar) direction. One thing was clear, however: this was not to be simply a *male* anthology. We would encourage and include submissions from women (among which we were to find much of the strongest work on the subject); we also talked about the possibilities of following up with a "Mothers" issue for *DT* 18.

Dacotah Territory 17, *Fathers*, was indeed published in late 1980, made possible by a grant from the Minnesota State Arts Board. We also used the occasion to publish one last chapbook—*The Bicycle in the Snowbank*, a lovely collection of poems by Mary Pryor. Mary also happens to teach in the MSU English Department, and her first volume of poems, *No Metaphysics*, had been part of our original chapbook series six years earlier. Once again, it seemed like we were ending where we had begun.

In spite of the successes of *Dacotah Territory* 16 and 17, we began to realize that we were changing, as were the times. Up to that point, funding had never been a real problem for the magazine, nor for the books (which tended to pay for themselves). We could be a bit proud of the fact that in 10 years of publishing we had received a total of only about 7200 dollars in grant money (three CCLM grants, one NEA grant, and one from the MSAB), or somewhere around 20 percent of our total budget. But we could also look back at our very good fortune. Whenever the money ran out we had been able to get a grant, and that indeed led to our philosophy: to make the magazine and other publications as self-sufficient as possible, to do all we could to keep from being heavily subsidized. Certainly our relationship with Moorhead State had a great deal to do with being able to maintain that course, as did our relationship with Plains and other distributors. But we had a companion philosophy too: to do all we could to get the magazine to the readers, and that meant keeping prices as low as possible. So, no complaints here; we've certainly had fewer money troubles than most of our contemporaries, and even as we watched in our 10 years postage and paper increase nearly five-fold, we always found the means to continue. The final tally: over 16,000 copies of the magazine in print, over 7,000 copies of books and chapbooks. And most of them have been sold and read!

Lest I forget, surely one of the important factors in the saleability of *Dacotah Territory* has come from artists and photographers in this region. From Bernel Bayliss' woodcut on the cover of *DT* 1, through photographs by Linda Hanson and Wayne Gudmundson and drawings by Jim Ver Doorn and Carol Smith, to name just a few, we've been fortunate in the artistic resources we've had to draw from, and in Grayce Ray's strong counsel in all matters regarding layout and design. True, Grayce and I have sometimes fought about covers the way we've fought about poems, but, as the mail we've received has indicated, *Dacotah Territory's* artistic record has certainly pleased a number of people—myself included.

So, in nearly every respect *Dacotah Territory* owes its identity to a particular region—that unique set of circumstances bounded by time and place—and even if we have achieved both national distribution and some sense of going beyond the "regional" in its narrower definitions, our ties have remained to the Midwest. Well over half of what we've published has been by Midwestern writers. In part, that's been a kind of repayment; in part, it's meant that we've maintained most of our early ideals regarding the health of literature tied to *place* and decentralized small press publication in America. But what we tried to do 10 years ago is also what we've tried to do throughout our history: to publish the best poetry we could find, no matter the geographical area, gender, age, or reputation of the authors; to look for the new and fresh yet at the same time to promote the old standards of quality and truth in literature; to reaffirm the principles of wonder and surprise in poetry, against mere fad or trend; to promote synthesis and cooperation among small presses in whatever ways we could.

But times have changed. For one thing, it's extremely hard to maintain a magazine for 10 years. I'm approaching the point where I began: time and energy have drained away. We may have survived a bit longer than the average life expectancy for a little magazine, but there simply comes a point when it's time to stop. And 10 is such a nice round number.

For another thing, it seems to me that a great deal has changed in the past few years in the American small press scene, sometimes for the worse. As the large and commercial presses publish less and less creative work, almost no experimental work, and very little that is not commercially marketable, there has been an increasing burden placed on small presses. This has led to some disturbing occurrences. I'm seeing more hustling now, more bickering and self-centeredness, more competition and less sharing and reinforcement. Partly that's inevitable, as the small press movement continues to grow and become even more decentralized—at a time when prospects for funding and distribution become increasingly uncertain. But there's also a new kind of commercialism, too often pitting vision against balance sheets, what's worth reading against what will sell. I don't yet feel like a dinosaur, but perhaps that day isn't all that far off. Like Plains Distribution, *Dacotah Territory* seems now more than ever a child of the 1970's. And who can begin to predict the 80's, and beyond?

So it's time to pack the bags for the last time, but knowing that most endings are also beginnings. As I mentioned at the outset, there have been so many heartening responses to *Dacotah Territory* in the last few months, so many encouragements to keep going in any way possible, to give the magazine over to new editors so at least the name and tradition can continue. But there's no question in my mind that we cannot do this. Many years ago I spent an afternoon with Trish Hampl and Jim Moore talking about the ending of *their* magazine, *The Lamp in the Spine*. Then it was *me* with the arguments of giving the magazine to someone else, and what they told me then is what I finally understand now, what Tom McGrath has had to understand about his *Crazy Horse*. In the most important sense, a magazine is not a *thing*, impersonal and intangible. No, it's a spirit, a particular sense of taste and judgement, and maybe even a vision—something that's ultimately non-transferrable.

While a part of me feels bad about removing an outlet for publishing in the Midwest, part of me also feels good that there are many more Midwestern magazines in existence now than when we started. That's the part of me that still believes that American small press has the ability to regenerate itself constantly, on its own terms. Transferring *Dacotah Territory* to someone else, then, would also be a denial of my basic sense of just what small press *is*.

So, we end as we began—with most of our ideals still intact, still gathered around my dining room table sorting through letters and poems. I'm still arguing with Grayce, laying plans with Joe, sharing ideas with my good friends and colleagues such as Bob Schuler, John Judson, and Ted Kooser. And my wife Betsy is still doing most of the typing: what *she's* had to put up with for 10 years! We've all given up something, to be sure, but then we've gotten a lot back, too. It's easy to forget the hysterical letters from rejected poets or ones who simply didn't like us, remembering instead all the *other* letters (and many, many more of them) filled with affirmations (how I wish I could indulge myself a bit further and print some of those letters, but there's just no way to handle it well). Likewise, it's becoming easy to forget the petty and self-seeking behavior of a few people and replace it with memories of the fine and decent and dedicated people who still form the vast majority of those associated with poetry and magazines and small presses in this country. Finally, though it saddens me to see both *Dacotah Territory* and Plains ceasing operations at the same time, there remain the thousands of books and magazines we've sold, the writers we've published and the audiences we've reached, the incredible good will we've encountered from so many—those we've encouraged and helped, and those who have helped and encouraged us.

12

As this essay comes to a close at last, I do realize that I've probably tried to cover too much ground, and, in so doing, I've mentioned too many names. But I'm also frustrated in knowing just how much and how many I've left out. Too much has happened for me to do any more than touch the highlights of *Dacotah Territory*, sprawling as that effort may seem. But within the sprawl of the years and my prose, there's still plenty left to sustain me for a long time, and enough good poems, too, to sustain our readers.

So *Dacotah Territory* ultimately stands or falls on what it's done, what it's published, and for now we won't even call that an *ending*, but a kind of metamorphosis. Who knows, maybe it will be back some day, in some new form. That's always a possibility. Or we might, as someone has suggested, call this final anthology the beginning of a kind of sabbatical from editing and publishing. Whatever we call it, for now, here is a sampling of 10 years of the magazine—not labeled as "the best of," for that term in itself seems to deny the spirit of *Dacotah Territory* and it invokes a competitiveness I don't think we've ever really had. Rather, this is an editor's choice—mine and Grayce's, with much help from Bob Schuler, George Roberts, Deb Keenan, Jim Moore (in a systematic way), and several others (who have encouraged the reprinting of a certain poem or poet). Perhaps the best term is this: a "gathering" of poems, many that have stuck with us over the voyage of the past 10 years and are in some way representative of what we've tried to accomplish with the magazine. And for all of you who have made the voyage with us, or some part of it, our thanks, our love, our best wishes—for the past and whatever it is that's to come.

July, 1981

Dacotah Territory 1, Bernel Bayliss

James L. White
1936-1981

Just as I was busy preparing the final *Dacotah Territory* manuscript for publication the news came of the death of a dear and beloved friend, Jim White. There is so very much to say, but at this point there is simply no way of saying it, beyond this: he was a wonderful poet and a wonderful man, one who wrote more eloquently than anyone I know of wounds and death—especially in the terrible setbacks of his last years, the remarkable way he made peace with himself and his friends.

Jim White was born in Indianapolis, received his BA in English from Indiana University and his MA in Literary Criticism from Colorado State. For several years he worked as a professional ballet dancer, then as a writer with Navajo people in New Mexico and Arizona. He came to Minnesota in 1971 to work in Poets in the Schools, concentrating on the Chippewa community and the editing of *Time of the Indian*, a magazine of children's poetry. He received a Bush Fellowship in Poetry in 1978, and his poems appeared in many magazines; his books include *Divorce Proceedings* (University of South Dakota Press), *A Crow's Story of Deer* (Capra Press), and *The Del Rio Hotel* (Territorial Press). In the spring of 1982, Graywolf will publish *The Salt Ecstasies*.

He was a clay dancer—how very much we will miss him. The words of that poem, and the following one from *DT 11* perhaps can serve for now as epitaph—what he knew so ironically and so well:

> Poetry is a sea loose in me
> with words at the last fathom
> exposing the blue despair.
>
> If a poem can buy salt
> it must speak of dying,
> that we are violated by clocks
> and exorbitant fees.
>
> A poem then must speak of afternoon rain,
> or pain from unreasonable dancing,
> and how in sleep we prepare for death.

Not A Little Magazine:
Plains Distribution, *Dacotah Territory,* and the Publishing Game
Joseph Richardson

One hot June afternoon in 1974 when the Plains Bookshop in Moorhead, Minnesota was desperate for customers, or even browsers, I was daydreaming while looking out our shop window. Across the street, at the Moorhead Post Office, I spotted a tall, balding man staring back at the store. After what seemed to be a long while, he coiled himself into the seat of his Mercury and drove across the one-way to park in front of the shop. After staring at the store a while longer, he released himself from the car, opened his trunk, and pulled out a large white Hammermill box.

That afternoon Mark Vinz sold the Plains Bookshop a full collection of *Dacotah Territory*—the first literary journal we stocked. Toward the back of the store, behind the book stacks, we had reserved a considerable amount of room (made possible by our inability to purchase more books) for a couch and coffee pot. We romantically believed that a true bookshop, one caring for ideas, books, and clientele, in that order, required a comfortable and relaxed atmosphere along with a full coffee pot. Mark became an avid fan of our couch and coffee section which was well populated with undercapitalized speed readers who, after a quick sampling of our new titles, would proceed to excite us with ideas while relieving us of coffee. The business became more a club than a store, and I, as manager, could find little reason to stay at the counter while the patronage was in back.

I will admit that at first I was more interested in the concept of decentralized publishing (a tenet of the free speech movement) and Mark's dedication and enthusiasm for *Dacotah Territory* than I was convinced of the magazine's literary merit. However, the longer I spent with Mark and the more I read, the more interested I became in poetry and those literary journals and publishing activities that are most commonly referred to as little magazines and small presses. Somehow I was less inclined then to equate quality with small presses and literary journals edited by writers than with large commercial publishing houses. The myth goes: if it is good it will sell. And, while I might have favored the small locally owned and operated bookshops over the chain store, I did not transfer the inclination to the publishing industry. How many people, unassociated with publishing and writing, know or can explain the difference between a New Directions or a Dell book? Very few who came to our bookshop could remember who published the titles they were looking for, and not one customer asked to see our Random House new titles list. Among the general reading public there is little knowledge of or loyalty to publishing firms. Who among us can remember which publisher was responsible for that book on winning through intimidation? Because few people recognize differences among the various large commercial publishing firms, those firms are not held accountable for what they publish. This is not the case with smaller literary publishers who depend more on their reputations to sell the few books they print. If a book on winning through intimidation were published by the North Dakota Institute for Regional Studies or by Territorial Press, the few who read their books would probably write the publisher off as being sleazy, if not irresponsible.

Our bookshop had never carried much in the romance or western line. We were emphasizing history, politics, drama, philosophy, and, with Mark Vinz's guidance, developing the strongest poetry section in town. All in the couch and coffee section of the store were sure that an alternative bookshop (in that it stocked hard-to-find books and magazines) would make a go of it. In an effort to promote the shop, Mark assisted us by lining up a poetry reading with the Poetry Outloud Project. The night of the reading, the store was jammed with people but we sold less than $150.00 worth of books. The further we went from highly commercial books—into obscure titles unavailable anywhere else in town—the worse off financially we became. Many idealists liked the concept of our store, but few bought books. The owner decided that she would close shop in December of 1974, only six months after we opened.

Mark and I had talked at length about the problem we were having in obtaining many of the titles for the shop and the problem many of the publishers had in reaching stores willing to stock their titles. It seemed to us that an organization that would promote and distribute small literary magazine and press titles might be supported through grants made by foundations, corporations, and arts agencies. From December 1974 to the following June we worked on setting up such an organization—The Plains Distribution Service, Inc. (the name Plains being the only remnant of the failed bookshop). Mark worked on contacting writers and publishers while I worked on organizational structure, proposal writing and fund raising. With the assistance of the National Endowment for the Arts, the North Dakota Council on the Arts, and the Northwest Area Foundation, the first Plains mail order catalog (The Plains Booklist) was released in November 1975 and we were ready to take and fill orders. Once again, all of us who were involved with the Plains Distribution Service (and there were many people from throughout the Upper Midwest) felt that an audience for contemporary literary publications like *Dacotah Territory* did exist, and that if we were able to provide solid resources for finding out about the publications and for obtaining them, we would sell many. We believed our strongest support would come from colleges, universities, and libraries. After seeing that we probably, once again, over-estimated the size of the existing audience we decided to go beyond the mail order and library exhibits in more actively promoting the publications. In 1977 we launched, with the support of the Dayton-Hudson Foundation, the Bush Foundation and a little assistance from arts councils, what we called our Plains Book Bus Project. The project, as the name indicates, was basically comprised of a book bus full of publications, traveling throughout a seven state area. People from colleges, libraries, or community arts councils along with writers festivals and conferences, would ask us to bring in an author of one of the titles to give a reading and a couple of writing seminars. With the Book Bus Project, Plains Distribution Service, Inc. grew to be one of the largest arts organizations in North Dakota and the largest independent literary organization working in the Upper Midwest. Yet Plains Distribution Service, Inc. ceased activities in 1981. We were forced to stop simply because we lacked financial backing.

State arts agencies withdrew support given us through the Affiliated State Arts Agencies of the Upper Midwest (ASAAUM) by changing their guidelines in such a way that no literary activity would qualify for their grants. Foundations that had initially given us money wanted to see our support base broadened through increased earned income (sales or fees for services) or through grants from new foundations. New foundations categorically rejected our proposals (while complimenting us on our presentation and quality programming) because they were unwilling to give grants to literary-related projects. Our sales were low. The support we initially believed would come from college and university English departments and libraries never materialized. It is the last fact that certainly frustrated and undermined our staff morale. All of the above factors quickly met in 1980 to force us to stop.

"Tell me, Mr. Richardson, how is poetry art?"
    —Executive Director of a large foundation listing as an interest, the arts.

"Wouldn't it be nice if all of the writing could be put in one large book."
Librarian at the American Library Association Convention, Detroit

"The Council on Foundations does not believe there are enough member foundations interested in literature to warrant a forum on the subject."
From a foundation representative who inquired about such a possibility.

I firmly believe that the lack of support for Plains is rooted in the same attitude which makes publications like *Dacotah Territory* so important and so short lived. The role of small literary magazines and presses in developing writers' talent has seldom been seriously questioned. How can it be underestimated when Henry Miller, Anais Nin, William Carlos Williams, Ernest Hemingway, Lawrence Durell, Ezra pound, Samuel Beckett, D.H. Lawrence, Hart Crane, Katherine Anne Porter, James Joyce, Gertrude Stein, Archibald MacLeish, Walt Whitman, T.S. Eliot, Virginia Woolf, and many more writers now recognized, before and after depended on the small literary presses for publishing their earliest and most experimental work. And many of the above writers were involved with publishing through editing their own magazines and presses, or volunteering their time as editors for someone else's press or magazine. Some even went so far as to publish their own work—a ghastly affair which we now call vanity publishing. Given this history, one would think that librarians and English profs would be delving through small literary publications looking for the next generation of writers, but this is not the case. In fact, librarians and English profs are, in my experience, most likely to resist small literary publications—turning instead to the commercially condensed anthology which has the power of annointing before the reading public and classroom those writers "worth reading."

The exhibition hall for the American Library Association Convention, held in Detroit, had closed for the night. I, like many other exhibitors, could be found in the nearest bar. Since I was alone and obviously listening to their conversation, two representatives of a large New York publishing firm asked if I would join them. Noticing, by my badge, that I was an exhibitor and representing Plains Distribution Service, Inc., one of the reps asked about our firm. I told him that Plains was a non-profit organization promoting and distributing small press literary titles from the Midwest. The rep leaned back in his chair and said, "Oh, I envy you." He added, "at least you sell books. We sell cans of corn in hardbound editions." Both of the representatives had majored in literature in college, both had felt that working with a large publishing house would provide them an opportunity to mix their literary interests with jobs. They had felt that occupations in publishing would allow them to be close to writing and writers. Instead, they were frustrated with hype—hype that sold what they considered to be of no greater value than another can of corn.

In 1959 Bennett Cerf and Donald Klopfer, owners of Random House, decided to open the ownership of that company through the formation of a corporation issuing stock to the public. This change was made, in large part, to avoid what could amount to a confiscatory inheritance tax if the value of the company were left to be determined by the Internal Revenue Service, upon the death of one of the partners. The Random House stock was well received and quickly sold. In 1960 Bennett Cerf offered Alfred Knopf, owner of the respected publishing house of the same name, cash and Random stock along with autonomy in management and editorial policy in exchange for ownership of Knopf. Random took over Knopf. As the stock market turned bullish, other publishing houses followed the Random House lead. Looking back at the decision to go public, Bennett Cerf, in his book *At Random* said: "This marked a big change, since the minute you go public, outsiders own some of your stock and you've got to make periodic reports

17

to them. You owe your investment dividends and profits. Instead of working for yourself and doing what you damn well please, willing to risk a loss on something you want to do, if you're any kind of honest man, you feel a real responsibility to your stockholders." Speculating, prematurely, that the electronic/computer textbook was about to take off and, therefore, publishing firms would enhance the holdings of electronic related corporations, RCA purchased Random House in 1966. With Random, RCA was also getting Modern Library and Knopf. RCA was not alone in what turned out to be a fever of acquisitions: ITT, even before RCA had acquired Random, scored Bobbs-Merrill; Litton Industries snapped up D. Van Nostrand; Gulf & Western bought the large paperback publisher Pocket Books and later Simon & Schuster; Holt, Rinehart & Winston, Praeger Publishing, Popular Library, and Fawcett all went to CBS; Xerox opted to purchase the major publishing trade resource R.R. Bowker Company (*Publishers Weekly, Books in Print,* and *Library Journal*). In order to compete for manuscripts and the efficiency that came with bigness, it seems that no serious commercial publisher wanted to be left out alone. Doubleday purchased Dell which had previously purchased Dial Press and Noble & Noble; Harper & Row purchased Basic Books, Barnes & Noble Publishing, Dodd, Mead College Division, and Thomas Y. Crowell; Time Inc. bought Little, Brown and Book-of-the-Month-Club—and the list goes on. The merger activity of the last twenty-five years has led to concentration in the publishing industry. What this concentration has meant to writers, publishers, editors, the book buying public, and, more importantly, the literature of this country is being hotly debated today and may depend upon your perspective.

Oscar Dystel, former chairman and chief executive of Bantam Books, stated in his speech at the Eighth Annual Richard Rogers Bowker Memorial Lecture, held November 25, 1980: "On balance the conglomerate experience with publishing has been mixed. Some corporate marriages will continue to be happy, but most, I fear, will not. Long-term sucess can only be achieved by maintaining publishing independence and editorial integrity. That demands flexible thinking many large corporations simply do not have." Nancy Evans' article for *Publishers Weekly* (July 31, 1978), entitled "How Authors are Affected," states: "Agents report that publishing houses have used whatever large sums of money they've been able to tap from parent companies to compete for big books. There has been no across-the-board incease in advances, agents are quick to point out. Instead, the marketplace for manuscripts has shaped up into a boom or bust situation. The big book wins an advance larger than ever while many books go begging."

When a publisher peels off a million dollar advance for one title, you can be sure that that publisher will do everything possible to get the money back fast. More copies of the book are printed and more advertising is required to sell the copies. If hype will return the investment, then hype it shall be. The flock approach to promotion tends to return the investment best. How many times have we noticed a whole flock of titles about natural catastrophes or psychological horror thrillers or space invasions by unworldly creatures hit the market about the same time? Publishers can work from current trends in the motion picture industry, television, and each other in milking fast sales with less advertising expense. Again, from Oscar Dystel's lecture: "… unhappily, I see less and less willingness to risk failure today, and an inclination more and more to bet on the tried and true; to follow what's left of innovation, not with more innovation, but with slavish imitation, until that last dollar has been squeezed from a promotional trend or editorial category that should have been buried long ago."

Publishing is, more than ever, a solid partner of the entertainment industry. The formula used by CBS in determining what shows might sell to a broad public, can not be all that different from that used by its subsidiary publishing house in deciding where it will place the big money—which novel will become the next best seller. I am not trying to imply here that the large commercial publishing houses no longer publish books of literary merit. I am saying that it happens less frequently, and when it does happen that they publish a writer's first novel which is of high literary merit, the chances that the novel will receive further support from the advertising and marketing department are indeed slim.

The most telling of Oscar Dystel's remarks before the Eighth Annual Richard Rogers Bowker Memorial Lecture is: "We should understand something of the agony inherent in the writing process, and we should even be able to work with writers if necessary." That advice, given to his publishing colleagues, would have been unnecessary many years back. It certainly demonstrates how far large commercial publishers have removed themselves from the craft they purport to present.

Obviously the two representatives I talked with during the American Library Association Convention had become disillusioned in discovering that publishing was far from what they had first believed. The commercially published book is, most often, a product of a large manufacturer which exists for the profit of its shareholders. Success is delivered in the form of larger dividends and a healthy appreciation of the corporate stock. What is profitable is not necessarily that which is of the highest quality—not in the chain restaurant, the film industry, nor the publishing industry. We understand the difference between commercial television and radio stations and their public counterparts, and, yet, we resist making the same distinction in publishing. This is most frustrating and disturbing when the resistance comes from those who are entrusted by the public to know the difference: English professors and librarians.

In contrast to the large commercial publishers, small literary presses and magazines are almost always run at a loss by writers who are not paid for their time. Without this dedication to every aspect of writing and publishing, it would be reasonable to believe that literature in the United States would suffer irrecoverably from a lack of depth, both in writers' talent and in the experimentation with form vital to keeping literature an art. And, without the dedication of those involved in magazines like *Dacotah Territory*, contemporary poetry, which has been written off by large publishing establishments, would be unavailable to even the small readership it currently enjoys. Look in any commercially published poetry anthology and you will discover that, with very few exceptions, all the work was first published in the small literary magazines.

In commenting on the role of small literary magazines, and especially *Dacotah Territory*, the regional significance can't be ignored. For those of us living in the Midwest, these small publishing ventures are, together with the university presses like the North Dakota Institute for Regional Studies, our major publishing houses. There is something ominous about having so much of what we read, or see on television or in movies, filtered through corporations located in Manhattan and Hollywood. We, in the Midwest, are different from those who grew up in New York or California. While working with Plains, I often had people refer to a certain author's book as being published in New York. They would not mention which publisher had published the book—that seemed not to matter. Being published in New York was somehow an indication that the book was of higher quality than one, say, that was published in Fargo. Being a writer from New York or a film director from Hollywood was a distinction of quality. While being from the outside is perhaps always viewed as being better, one can't help but wonder how the concentration of publishing, television, and film in two small geographical areas has contributed to a Midwestern inferiority complex that prevents us from taking ourselves seriously as writers and artists. I had heard, on several occasions, writers and editors say that they considered *Dacotah Territory* to be one of the best literary magazines in America. Yet, it was often difficult to sell copies in North Dakota or South Dakota because, I believe, it was perceived as being local and therefore inferior. Plains Distribution Service attempted to carry Midwestern publications to Midwestern readers, not in an effort to be exclusive of those publications produced outside of the region, but to complement what was more readily available—which was often from outside the region. It was (and some of us used to joke around about it) easier to obtain works by Midwestern writers and publishers in New York than it was to obtain them within the region. To hear *ourselves*—or to hear those among us who are geographically connected—is necessary to develop our own image of ourselves in relation to a broader universe. *Dacotah Territory* was an extremely strong magazine on this count. It attempted to bring in writing from outside the region and place it alongside that produced inside the region, thereby giving us in one literary magazine the ability to review or look for any distinction between "regional" and "national" poetry. While *Dacotah Territory* was editorially joining regional and national, Plains' job was to deliver *Dacotah Territory* and other Midwest publications to the region's audience. In that way, Plains and *Dacotah Territory* worked well together—not as a provincial, regionalist project, but as projects of and for the region. The *real* provincial attitude is the one that allows Manhattan and Hollywood through default to define our image of ourselves.

Had it not been for *Dacotah Territory*, Mark Vinz would probably not have spent so much time in the coffee and couch section of the Plains Bookshop, nor would he and I have come together in the creation of Plains Distribution Service, nor would we have been able to help provide (with the rest of the American small press scene) alternatives to the conglomerate approach to publishing and distribution which has the potential of damaging both a healthy sense of region and literature in general. In turn, Plains has been the source for many activities, which *will* carry on. From one small literary magazine, so much has come and will continue to ripple out.

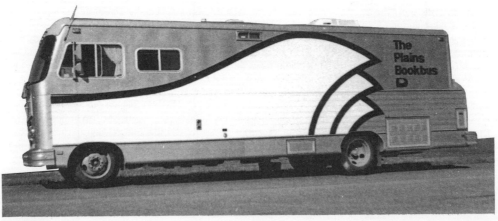

Leo Kim

Entering Dacotah Territory

Robert Schuler

At Rochester land and sky seethed together, a swirling wall of snow. Several cars, their headlights barely visible, slid past me, both on my right and my left. I was on the wrong side of the freeway. I had to get off—I turned left on the first road I spotted. Damn, it wasn't an entrance but an exit ramp, and a semi with a trailer was grumbling toward me. I couldn't stop in time, I couldn't turn off, so I headed for the snow drifted thickly against the railing. The snow cracked as I banked and whomped round the trailer, nicking its last mudflap with my rear bumper. The steering wheel and my arms streamed sweat.

On the other side of the hill: more visibility, no traffic. A simple U-turn and I was on my way again.

January, 1975. I was travelling from Illinois to serve as a visiting professor in a seminar on Politics and Literature at a small Minnesota liberal arts college. After sliding down ice-coated back roads for a few hours, I arrived, pale, nervous, but on time for class, received a short introduction from a colleague, and set to with Malraux's *Man's Fate*.

At noon the radio announced that the blizzard was a major one: many had died in stalled, stranded vehicles, a woman snowmobiler had been beheaded by barbwire, roofs had collapsed, smothering inhabitants. At the college, afternoon classes and all other activities had been cancelled. Although circumstances dictated finding a bar for a prolonged drinking session, I had to see more of the storm. I walked for several hours, most likely in circles. Gusts nearly knocked me down. Here and there I could see dimly the outlines of a roof or a chimney, trees disappearing into the wind. Suddenly, a small, frosted wall of light.

Still open for some reason, the campus bookstore was crowded with customers. While browsing, I was struck by the cover of a magazine stacked on the right of the tiny poetry shelf. The cover seemed to have been photographed earlier that day: a line of cows streched across fathomless white. In hand, the magazine, *Dacotah Territory 5*, felt curiously weighty. A warm, earthy, stone-gray format. Inside poems by Bly, Stafford, and a host of unknowns (unknown to me at least). Just one dollar. Why not? The cover alone was worth it.

That evening, while planning the next day's seminar, I was often distracted by the cows treading through the storm. Finally, I grabbed a brandy and started to read the damn magazine, just to get it out of my system. Bly and Stafford were good, as expected. The unexpected was even better: Maggie Sversvold's "December 17," Patricia Hampl's "The Marsh at Boy River," James Fawbush's "Driving Home from Park River," Rory Holscher's "Mississippi Valley Slowdown." Well crafted, the poems were grounded in detailed landscapes, but none of them were limited to mere description; most rose into other dimensions. For instance, Holscher's excellent poem (still a personal favorite) ends with the lines,

> I knew an old man who kept sharpening one knife
> til he handled a blade thin as starlight.

Dacotah Territory 5 was impressive; indeed, inspiring: the crystallized images, the high level of poetic craft, the discrimination of the editor, Mark Vinz, the clean, unpretentious format. Next morning I bought the first four issues.

When I returned to my own campus, I strengthened my poetry course by assigning more work by Midwestern poets, including several issues of *Dacotah*. My students began to make their own hunts for good contemporary poets and to present their discoveries in inspired, border-shattering classrooom sessions. I began to dream about publishing my own magazine.

My encounter with *Dacotah* seemed fated. During the summer of 1974, my wife had dragged me off to a Wisconsin lake for a three-week vacation. Reluctant, I had planned the usual academic and administrative duties, but clearly I was unusually exhausted, depressed, desperately in need of a break. Her decision was a wise one, for that summer I learned again, after too many years of dwelling in mind and ego, just how much I needed to live close to the land. I took up fishing again, canoed, hiked, spent twelve curing hours a day out of doors. After our return to Illinois, I walked every day over the wooded knolls and the palisaded streams. At night I tried clumsily to capture in poems the images that had captured me.

After January, I felt even more at home. Not only had the *Dacotah* writers, to follow an Hasidic image, thrown more sparks back into the woods, they had proved to me that a fine poetry of place was possible; yes, even highly desirable.

My first published poem, loosely based on my drive through the blizzard, was published that fall.

In January, 1976, two of my students, Terry Nathan and John Nausieda, raised money to operate a literary journal, *Uzzano* (named after one of the many mysterious heros in Pound's *Cantos*, a key book in my poetry classes). Their first two issues featured poems by Stafford, McGrath, Keith Gunderson, and Franklin Brainard. In June, to my great surprise, they gave me the journal, a small subscription list, and a few hundred dollars. The first issue of *Uzzano* under my editorship was a memorial edition of Franklin Brainard's poetry. Again, a line back to *Dacotah Territory 5*, which had offered a review of Brainard's *Raingatherer*, a marvelous volume of poems. I had ordered that book immediately and, shortly afterwards, had invited Brainard to Illinois for a reading. Frank read vibrantly for six hours that day to hundreds of students, teachers, and townspeople. I hoped the memorial edition would pass on to others Frank's generous gift to us.

In time came contact with some of the Midwest's finest writers and the opportunity to publish collections by Thomas McGrath, John Knoepfle, Dave Etter, Ray Smith, and Todd Moore (to name a few whose work I met in issues of *Dacotah*). Six *Uzzano* books were selected to appear in the Plains Distribution Service (a visionary arm of *Dacotah*) booklist and were carried by the Plains Bookbus on its lumbering literary pilgrimages through the off-the-map small towns of the midwest. Baskets of letters and manuscripts, many close friendships (I often believe I belong to a medieval guild), talks fueled by poems and wine—the results of my entry into Dacotah Territory continue.

Somewhere along the way, *Dacotah* accepted some of my poems.

Thanks, Mark Vinz, and Grayce Ray, and all of the guest editors. Six of my best years, ten grand ones for *Dacotah Territory*, and more to come.

June 1981

Confessions of An Associate Editor, or, Exit Smiling, Stage Left

Grayce Ray

A ten year accumulation of *Dacotah Territory* stacks up to a rather small pile. When I first encountered Mark at Moorhead State it was after several people had assured me that he would know where poetry was happening. (Indeed, they might have gone further and told me he was one of the main reasons poetry was alive in this particular stretch of the Red River Valley at all!) At any rate, there was Mark across from Tom McGrath's office. The ubiquitous scraps of paper pinned to the door with yellowed Doonesbury cartoons, a post card, some photos and a heap of papers for grading marked the entrance. Inside a tall, stoop-shouldered, slightly balding man with a brown beard and deep set eyes peered over a desk and an avalanche of more paper, books, post cards and fat brown envelopes. Around him paperbacks heaped bookshelves and spilled onto window ledges and the floor. That first conversation escapes me now, but I do remember feeling a great sense of excitement—a sense that there was indeed a writing community here and that Mark Vinz was marking out the boundaries of a forgotten land. Sometime later I returned and we began the work of redesigning the magazine that was three issues old at the time.

Mark is a little more bald and a little more stooped. The piles of paperbacks have grown, there are still papers to be graded outside the office door. The chubby, rosy cheeked infant that sprawled in the snapshot on his desk is taller than I am now. The magazine is now many issues old, and beside that stack we could lay several anthologies and chapbooks. It is time to pause and take stock.

Dacotah Territory is Mark's magazine. That there have been guest editors from time to time has not altered the focus of the magazine. It is a poetry magazine. . .its purpose to publish the best poetry we could find without reference to the writer's being an established poet or an unknown. Simply that he (or she) be a writer and, in our judgement, have written a sound piece. True, at first there was an emphasis on "regional" work because we felt that there was really no place for the writer in this particular place /area/ region to deal with the reality of the "mid-west." Very quickly we found that good writers were alive and productive in this region—but we also found hundreds of fine manuscripts coming from across the country dealing with a sense of place and space.

One rather charming inquiry I received asked earnestly whether the U.S. Midwest experience differed much from the Canadian Midwest experience. That question in its way underscored our decision to move in a wider direction and we began to accept poems from everywhere. Norwegian translations, Spanish translations, poems from Ireland, England, New York. Sometimes they would come tumbling out of the envelope and literally dazzle us. Other times they fell with a resounding thunk onto the desk. Occasionally, there were others that rang true for the most part but were unfinished and we would begin a sometimes lengthy correspondence with the writer to try to smooth out the clinkers. Again I remember one note from a poet who wrote "I know that the poem isn't finished yet. What do you think I should do with it now?" Of course we refrained from telling her just what we did think.

Sometimes we were able to write personal notes to the poets we accepted/rejected, but not for long. There was always too much mail, too many manuscripts. Resorting to a printed rejection slip hurt us but was a necessity. Even so there were angry responses from writers who were really looking for a teacher /mentor/ muse. One such was a series of letters from an enraged would-be poet who was certain that not only was I illegitimate but that we had a personal reason for suppressing his work. At such times we resisted the urge to reply ala *Esquire:* "Dear Sir: This is not the kind of shit we are currently eating." Some of those letters later turned up refined and tuned to a sharp edge in Mark's collection for Capra Press, *Letters to the Poetry Editor*. You find yourself doing strange things after poems have been coming across your desk with regularity en masse…things like writing about writing, writers and editing, and editors. Maybe it's a response to all those personae that people your nightmares with postage due or no S.A.S.E., or painfully revealing bits of the writer embedded. I don't know.

Making the final decision about accepting the poem has often been a stand-off. We've argued, fought, cajoled, horse-traded, refused to have anything to do with poems sent by personal friends, but always tried to make the decision based upon the merits of the poem itself. Again, according to our best judgement. Surprisingly too, Mark and I are still friends *and* most importantly, the poems have for the most part stood up to the years. I know that because going through the past issues for this anthology was painful. So many poems grabbed me with the same freshness, the same strength as when we first met them.

Limitations. There was never enough space for all the submissions, postage kept rising along with paper and printing costs. We didn't have an office *again!* We didn't have enough time for editing/proofing/press running/collating/mailing. Gritty eyes at midnight going over the typeset copy, inkstained fingers after hours running the press, cranky kids corraled to collate (excuse the alliteration, it just happened). And funds, always funds.

We were lucky too. Betsy, Mark's wife, and her flying fingers and sharp eye and cookies and coffee. Her tolerance of the mess on the dining room table (and floor), her patience with the harangue going on over manuscripts 'til all hours, and her typing and proofing and mailing and feeding and care for us. The bills that were paid by the bookstores in time to pay for another mailing. Subscriptions from all over, including my favorite from Sydney, Australia.

Finally we were lucky to have the support of other editors and poets. They encouraged, sent work from promising poets, sent money and exchanged solutions they had worked out for publishing small press. Several Writers Conferences brought us together with other poets/editors and contributed a sense of shared mission. Tom McGrath and Dick Lyons, Steve Ward and Joe Richardson right here at hand lent time and support. So many poets in so many places gave us so much. I like to think we gave some of it back with *Dacotah Territory*.

Going back through the ten-year accumulation of the magazine has been bitter-sweet. There are names on the contributors' list for those who are gone. Some friends, some friendly strangers known briefly in a few typed lines, will not write again. Poetry is a hard mistress and cold comfort sometimes too. She exacts from one his best and too often gives no reward. When *Dacotah Territory* began, Jim White had just published his first collection. Jim died last month. When we first began the magazine some newly married couples were also just beginning. Too many of them have separate addresses now and children have become scattered young men and women who were then impatient little ones.

I have learned much of my craft from the magazine. Being exposed to the best (and the worst) of poetry happening here and now for ten years has opened doors and let the wind of time blow in. When it did, it brought with it rumor of war, chances for peace, skewed perspective on interior landscapes, rage and sometimes, love. For this I am grateful. For the friends *Dacotah Territory* has made I am truly thankful. It has been worth the hours and wrinkled forehead, and I honestly can say that if we decide to do it all again sometime, I haven't learned to say No. . .even with the paper cuts still stinging on my fingers there is a particular singing in my heart when I look at what we've accomplished.

Post script:
Let me assure the reader of the above that the piles of paper outside Mark's office door have not remained static. They are constantly renewing themselves in a rather Sisyphus-like manner. Grading, like death and taxes, is certain as long as one continues to teach.

In spite of the very serious nature of much of this article I cannot resist including a couple of *editor* type poems from our experience. It is well to remember that they were written with tongue firmly in cheek and it also should be pointed out that Mark almost never permitted me to print any of his work in *DT* before this. However, this is my piece. He has no say, just this once.

IV. Dear Shithead:
This makes 14 poems y've
rejected this spring alone.
The shit you print reflects
yr taste. It's eds. like
yourself who ruin it all &
I just hope yr pleased.

(p.s. enclosed find
five new poems)

XIV. Dear Editor,
Even though I've never been
west of the Hudson River
I feel a strong kinship for
the Great plains. There are
barns & blizzards in these
poems, & lots of Indians.
Do you see many of these,
where you are?

(Both of the above are from *Letters to the Poetry Editor*, Mark Vinz, published by Capra Press, 1975.)

Finally, one of my own poems written in a fit of pique after a long session:

EDITOR'S LAMENT

Since word went out upon the wires
The manuscripts have found me.
In plain brown envelopes,
Pink, perfumed, thick vellum,
Anemic onionskin, folders of manila
With postage due, and overweight.
Unsolicited but shamelessly soliciting.
The mailbox has overflowed, the hallway is stacked.

Last week I nailed the mail slot shut
The postal authorities called to forbid it
With injunctions and depositions
and one subpoena which fell into
The laundry basket overflowing with letters.

The refrigerator chills poems from lovers.
The dryer holds those from suicides by drowning.
42 Eskimo poems by a Jewish mother in Brooklyn
Pop out of the bread box twice daily.
The aquarium is dry—two dead piranha
And 80 sonnets on prairie landscapes.
Threatening poems (written in block capital letters
cut from newspapers)
Are held down by five bricks in the celler.

Dacotah Territory

1— January 1971 (cover by Bernel Bayliss, drawings by Tim Hagen)
2— February 1972 (cover and drawings by Tim Hagen)
3— Summer 1972 (guest edited by Thomas McGrath; cover and drawings by David Parsons)
4— Winter-Spring 1973 (cover and graphics by Paul Wong)
5— Summer-Fall 1973 (guest edited by Thomas McGrath; cover and photographs by Linda Hanson)
6— Winter 1973-74 (Native American issue, guest edited by James L. White; cover and graphics by Jim McGrath)
7— Spring-Summer 1974 (cover and graphics by Jim Howard)
8/9— Fall-Winter 1974-75 (cover by Terry Mahnke; drawing by Carol Smith; photograph by Jeff Carter)
10— Spring-Summer 1975 (edited by Grayce Ray; cover and graphics by Richard Dokken)
11— Fall 1975 (Minnesota Poets in the Schools issue; cover by James Ver Doorn)
12— Winter-Spring 1975-76 (cover by Dale Amundson and Charlotte Werner)
13— Fall 1976 (Sixth Anniversary issue; cover by Linda Hanson)
14— Spring-Summer 1977 (cover and graphics by Carol St. Clair)
15— Winter-Spring 1977-78 (cover by Carol Smith)
16— Winter 1979-80 (Hotel and Cafe Poems and Photographs; cover by Jerry Anderson; 16 photographs edited by Wayne Gudmundson)
17— Winter 1980-81 (Fathers; cover by James Ver Doorn; photograph by Wayne Gudmundson; drawing by Gaylord Schanilec)

Chapbook Series

1973— James Fawbush, *Great Grandpa Nettestad Was Blind*
Dale Jacobson, *Dakota Incantations*
Robert Waldridge, *From A Place Which Is No Longer Named*

1974— Grayce Ray, *The River Is Always Straight Ahead*
Michael Moos, *Hawk Hover*
David Martinson, *Bleeding the Radiator*
Mary Pryor, *No Metaphysics*

1975— Antony Oldknow, *Anthem for Rusty Saw and Blue Sky*
Richard Lyons, *Racer and Lame*
David Solheim, *On the Ward*

Other Books

1974— Thomas McGrath, *Voices from Beyond the Wall*
1975— James L. White, *The Del Rio Hotel: New and Selected Poems*
1976— James L. White, editor, *The First Skin Around Me: Contemporary American Tribal Poetry*
George Roberts, *The Blessing of Winter Rain*
1980— Mary Pryor, *The Bicycle in the Snowbank*

Jenne Andrews

Turning With The Ears Of The Horse

Tonight the winds of a red moon
touch the horse's golden flank,
warm after running
and lift my hair again
after the loss of childhood fields.
There is a falling away
of bone-deep memory.

Over the barn jets come in,
dropping through rivers of night turbulence
to the cold breadth
of runways nearby.

There is no ownership here
in the return of silence,
or in the collective musk
of the hay.
And the moon-bright gelding we share
shares himself in return,
carrying the heart forward.

The tractor stands with its ear to the dark
like an iron cricket belonging to all.
And when I touch my horse's luminous mane
we move through the mist
between ourselves and other things
like explorations of love and fire
on a pale curtain.

Noreen Ayres

Turncoat

It's been done before—
poets and suicide.
No good following that act.

    All those years I had it planned,
    all those years of something in reserve,
    the trick up the sleeve.

I never could stand to read a paragraph over.

Plath dissolved my dream
and Alvarez with his goddamned book,
that death is always blue and nasty,
it's always got bugs in it.

Cancel, cancel, cancel.
That was my prerogative.

    Now all my arguments for death
    look foolish as a nun bowing to the east.

Kate Basham

At A Retrospective Of Chinese Art

Lost in the gull fog of digestion
the grandmother sails in ships of gray hair.

They are waiting in line.
Her sisterinlaw says to the guard,

This woman is dying of cancer. Do you think
she wants to stand around here all day?

He gets her a wheelchair and lets them through.
She knows all boats are equal when any boat will do;

all nets are nets of imprecision.
A retrospective is like wallpaper

in a house: everywhere the same boats,
the same wind in the sails, the same race.

Robert Bly

Driving Toward Dacotah Territory
for Tom McGrath

Between the road and the sky there is a bare ashtree!
It looks like the arteries inside an old man's head,
or the diagram of the spirit of an Indian.

The immense and fiery west
hovers over the water towers of the small towns ahead!
The sun is still lighting Paynesville,
turning the concrete steps of the teller's house a soft pink.

But the boxelder groves are growing dark,
and the dry leaves
growing triumphant with the night that is invading!
There will be dances tonight:
William Jennings Bryan will return tonight in those leaves,
there are already tiny whirlpools moving over them,
not noticed by the farmer who drives past
on his tractor, seeing work gloves lying on a kitchen table.

Telephone poles pull night out of the ground
and pass it over to the sky.

The pale blue sky, the color of Christian pity,
leads far away, away, from the earth.

The day is over and the night come.
The first gas-station lights have been turned on.

Late Moon

The third week moon reaches a light over my father's farm.
Half of it is gone now, in the West that eats it away.
The earth has rocks in it that hum at early dawn.
I turn to go in, and see my shadow reach for the latch.

Thinking of "Seclusion"

I get up late and ask what has to be done today.
Nothing has to be done, so the farm looks doubly good.
The blowing maple leaves fit so well with the moving grass.
The shadow of my writing shack looks small beside the growing trees.

Never be with your children, let them get stringy like radishes!
Let your wife worry about the lack of money!
Your whole life is like some drunkard's dream!
You haven't combed your hair for a whole month!

Franklin Brainard

The Edge of Boundaries

Ears sieve many soundings
choosing meets and bounds
whose borders never stay in place:
bent birds in rocky breaks of air,
dry mountains and dry sage
reflected from mirages that fade,
yellow and white butterflies
over the purple flowers of August clover.
Granite never grows impatient
but the robes of Job change more than Jacob's
and lo, we see them on our shoulders.

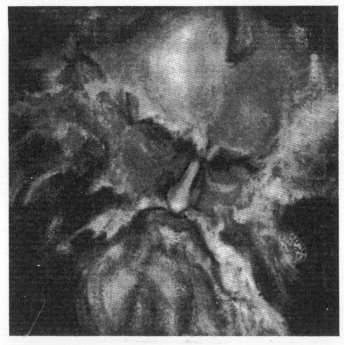

Dacotah Territory 17, James Ver Doorn

Michael Dennis Browne

Captain Cat

My cat has no desires.
He could sleep for a hundred years.
Captain Cat. Captain Castrati.

He climbs a tree & thinks
he's an owl. He is, he is.
He floats to my hand,
there is a candle in his claw.

My cat has no desires.
Aloft in the garbage he strums
the harp of the dead fish.
He is not in the snow,
he is in Mexico.

Captain, when you wake
in a hundred years,
stretch, yawn,
do all the things that you do.
We will be here, the dog & I,
by the fire.
It is only snow coming down
through the open roof.
And soon we will fix you some supper.

Bad Poems

Bad poems are lying around
in huge jugs; I will not drink them!
I take a piece of beer
& nail it to the sky.
Driving, I see a nun crossing the road
& step on the gas-pedal, & get her;
these bad poems will disguise themselves
as anything!
I wake one morning
with cobwebs between my thighs;
I rush to the bathroom—
the dentures of hundreds of bad poems
piled in the bath-tub.
That night, when I switch on
my lamps, bad poem moths
storm them again & again,
as if there were a sale on light.
And just when I can begin
to forget, to concentrate, the phone goes
it is a whole troop of giggling
bad poems on the other end,
and they are calling, of course, Collect.

William Burns

Alcoholic: The Morning Beckon

I open a door on his Paramount stare.
It's theatre grey at five a.m.
Doubled over, he's hooked in his chair,
Evenly maimed. What's playing on the floor,
X rating the litter, is what the cat
Dragged in for hours, in dreams, twitchy
As he. I'm smooth with logic, spoon feed
Honey, and AA, slick as a swear off.
He's tight lipped, deep in his dive.
Above his shoulder, tilted back
In shelved debris, his bottle rides
His crash like a wave; where everything topples
Is Tipsy Swill, hoarded for glory.
Offset, tripped up on his ragged edges,
My Twelfth-Step call fails like a pipsqueak.
She's ready, harbor breathed, curved
As Circe, her slopes pushy as swine.
There's glint in her glass sty. His lurch
Is true blue, her winey mouth
All summons. Her promise crooks like a finger.
Tugging, his memories fill like sails.
His cup runneth over and over.

John Caddy

Sharing The Cry

We cannot name this sound.   It locks the jaw.
It curls the tongue into the shapes
of sucking marrow from the bone.

From the pines a scream across the lake,
at first a woman's scream—but more, no hint of fear,
an endless wailing high and sliding down at last
to break on teeth and tongue,
a celebration of the lungs,
a chilling song from somewhere wet and warm,
with overtones of spit and fur.

It shocks the muscles cramped,
leaves hands clamped tight around the paddle's shaft,
and leaves the ear dazzled like the eye
by splintered waves reflecting light.

We cannot name this cry,
but know that this was animal, raw, entire,
and through the leaping drum of heart and ear,
the texture on our skins of standing fur,
we slowly realize that this was cougar's scream.

After, we hear no sound, make none.
Our faces pale, scanning trees, we watch
a heron lumber out of reeds, getting out of there.
We drift in the canoe, and try to breathe.
We smile, and know one meaning of alive.

There are no cougars left up here, they say.
Does echo drain the marrow from the bone?
We know what's real: this cry
which strains our jaws to silence,
and echoes in our hollowing an old taut-sinewed fear
from the open throat of time.   Without this cry
which curls the tongue into such shapes as these,
we are shrunken.   With it, we are more.

Alvaro Cardona-Hine

Two Poems From the Garden

1.	2.
the	if
snail	dragon
climbed	flies
to	made
the	honey
top	their
of	honey
the	would
hill	be
	blue
the	and
turtle	you
dreamt	would
of	have
a	two
very	whole
small	jars
lover	of
	it

Christmas Eve

two hoboes
bending over a flame
in a field of inert weeds

heaven upstairs

the little broth of a train
in the distance
boiling down to nothing

Marisha Chamberlain

The Stars Are Apple Clusters

Exhaustion builds a maze of branches
behind my eyes the first day
I pick apples.   Day's end, my hands

still reach to pick.   Like gloves
gone threadbare, gloves with holes
I put those hands away

in my pockets. Darkness unleashes stars
and I connect them in dark trees: the leaping
impulse of my hands toward studded

branches.   A dream smears me apple red
and apple green.   I straddle a dozen
gleaming ladders, rolling apples

into my mouth to collect in my half-bushel
stomach with the trap door chute
to a crate big as an empty city.

Night falls down on my head like a tarp.
I rip a hole in the night
and reach up to pick the stars.

Art Cuelho

A Drifter's Brand

Long road dreams,
clouds in whiskey nights,
young boots tapping out old blues;
my name could be Utah,
Rainy Hunger, Lost Train;
my initials might be found
on a Great Northern boxcar.
But don't strain yourself stranger.
You can just call me Art.

Old hard to find rainbows,
beauty on a lonesome day,
thunder shattering a farmboy sigh;
that's me: my life is outlaw faith,
a river poem, thirst searching.

I am hitch-hiker salvation,
a thumb in the cold wind,
a diesel ride across the
Nevada Desert at midnight.
My suitcase as battered as
the bums of the dustbowl;
my palms know heart-broken
songless prairies howling
a drifter's brand—
no home no land.

My dark eyes hold no peace,
like a black man who dares to speak
I'm gonna saddle me up some relief.

Carl Cunningham

Ropes From Sky

I walk
on river sands, on the sound
giving water its foam,
holding on to the cries of crows.
They hold; and should
some slip of hearing break
the strand, I would fall from
a higher place. They would
fly across river, the faint specks
of being lost in vegetation haze, in
the weariness of sight, their
calls too low for ears: only
the long wash of a river
drinking all, leaving sand and foam
silence. And everywhere the earth-
rubbing circle of the great cry beyond hearing, told by the salmon
crows, those weavers of audible ropes
from earth to sky.

Philip Dacey

Bedtime Song

To sleep in the house of children,
In the house that children sleep in,
Is to sleep in the arms of children's
Dreams, that are dreaming the house,
And to dream you are the children
That are sleeping themselves into dream.

And to sleep in that house is to sleep
In the children, who are the house,
Who are the dark you sleep in
And the arms that hold you asleep,
And to dream in that dark is to house
The children, and you, for the night.

To sleep in a house that dreams
Children is to sleep well, to arm
Yourself for the night is to sleep
In the childish dark, and to dream
Of waking is to waken the child
Who is yourself, dreaming

Of sleep in the children's house.

D.W. Donzella

These Spring Girls

She waits in a fast looking car
for a boyfriend to bring back hamburgers.
Something is beautiful here:
the way she looks in denim,
and when the car door opens
the way she radiates legs.

Maybe she wants the boy,
or the night,
or the warmth of food on her knees.
Young is what you have
before you think of having.

At seventeen I took one like her,
took us both away from nights stuck between school
and days spent waiting for these nights,
drove her around in a car of my own
up and down until she had to be home
and wash her hair for tomorrow;
showing me what she went through
while I slept
or threw records over my ears.

I married her and sold the car
and learned to get the things
I can hold on to.

B. Doyle

The Diving Horse Act

Poppa said Shit!
wudja look at that.
And it was no stallion standing there.
"Shoshone"
lofty on his wooden tower.
A broken show pony
is more like it.
Even I knew that and
I might have believed it
nine years old
—waiting for the show.
Ignominy!
is all that pop could say
Use a horse so bad—
treat a horse like that's a sin
I'd swear it! on Crockett
by Hickok and Saint James.
Jesse's teeth! they treat a horse so bad.
He dove before the crowned heads
and splashed 'em fine
for god's sake.
Fools! and listen to them.

Horse atop a tower
wonder what he sees
gotta jump into a tub
to please the crowd of me
          and poppa

(it's his fault)
he took me here when no one else came.
Horse atop a tower
wonder if he needs
that bathing beauty
          on his back
squeezing with her knees.

Joseph Duemer

The Burning of the Ozark Hotel

The ones that woke to fire
hung out the windows like laundry
or ghosts. The ones who died in their sleep
are quiet—unidentifiable, even by experts.
Haunted by flames, the walls too hot to touch,
this woman dead on the sidewalk
dove for the cool window. Wearing what's left
of her nightgown she is trying to rise
through stories of smoke she dreams are clouds.
She must try to recapture
the sound of her scream as she fell
but her tongue is a streak of blood.
Her white blouses, untouched, hover in the closet
waiting for dinner at a daughter's.
In the coffee shop across the street
an old man whispers to himself
that he's alive: he knows tonight
he will dance with the one who fell, help her
forget the air and the embarassment of the dead,
how they picked her up with the other gutted stuff—
He will lift her like a wife, wheeling,
light-headed, barely touching
the icy floor of the moon.

Stephen Dunn

Palominos

In Manhattan, when the flies gathered
around the mouth of a wino, sticking
in the muscatel on his chin and dying,
I was feeding a palomino
I have always been feeding a palomino;
when the tanks rolled in Athens a palomino
I had borrowed from a statue ate the last
of my chocolates,
in Spain when the Guardia raised his machine gun
I was feeding a palomino though my hands appeared
to be reaching into the air;
I could do it in my sleep
in a room half the size of a palomino
if I had to, it's a luxury
the way escaping through the window
of an office that never existed
is a luxury only men who feed palominos really know.
Can you understand?
Beneath my shirt where my heart once was
a small orphaned palomino moans
when women slip their hands inside; this
is his only food, and he hasn't been eating well lately.
Once in Aruba the dark hands of a prostitute
turned him into a stallion,
and in Denver one cold afternoon I tried
feeding him with my own hands, but he knew
the difference, bit at my shirt, bit at
my invisible palomino monogram, left me naked,
open to ridicule.
But I would never stop feeding palominos;
at dinner last night, in that peculiar silence
that follows burnt vegetables, overdone beef,
several palominos licked my fingers
beneath the table. One of them was pregnant,
she ate like a horse, and I climbed on her
and she took me for a ride where other palominos were
and the dinner became meaningless
and I loved my wife.

That is what palominos will do for you
if you feed them, it is their special dignity,
their hunger for the loose hay we all have
lying around.
Right now there are carrots in my pocket
that look like palominos would love them
if the occasion ever arises,
but here on this farm outside of Syracuse
things are so quiet, the summer is practically over
and there is a palomino out back
who is so real I must feed her every day,
happy or not. She is very beautiful.
But she cannot be counted on in emergencies.

South Jersey Pastoral

As we pass by on wheels
the obsolescent horses never look up
and the cattle fold their legs
and say their calm So what.
What do we care,
everything is languorous, perfect:
even the slaughterhouses
are silent in the middle west
of our hearts, the sun is out
and a white moon
lingers like hope. It seems
we will live forever!
To our left, vineyards and winery.
The egg farm, the flea market.
Then the ocean, a wave cresting
far off shore, gulls riding it
who believe it breaks
because they move their wings.

Constance Egemo

The Keeper

the day is grey and windy
no one put away the milk
I am a good mother
the keeper of my husband's house
the keeper of the milk
the keeper of the long day
when he left there were tears in his eyes

when the children don't cry there's silence
no one put away the milk
the wind has an empty sound
my first child has three cowlicks like my husband
she has skin the color of milk
the blueness of her veins shines through
it is too late to plant flowers

the day is grey and windy
I try to start the car
the generator goes "click click"
I am a good mother
the keeper of my husband's house
the keeper of the long day
I am trapped in the house

there are chrysanthemums in my neighbor's garden
she is away all day
I hear the wind in the pitcher
I am a good mother
but I try to start the car
the generator goes "click click"
there were tears in his eyes as he left

my daughter has skin the color of milk
my sons have hair like their father
I love them with all my heart
but I have no garden
I am the keeper of the grey day
on my breast I might wear roses
were it not for the empty wind

William D. Elliott

By the Sea, I Speak of Winter

                    And before that last hour
its snow red with seaweed
the waves of Falmouth
shot like grapes into white rain
by the Amusement Park.
Crabs bloomed; the blank ice melted
all on the sea side of the new year,
all the last light of the Nantucket buoy.
We were deep in an open boat. The land was out of sight.
In a dry cold two bluefish answered off the glazed bow
flipped into the beard of sun, spoke like lions of the iced paws.
New Year's and the land was out of sight. Tonight was my last night.

                    By morning the crab
damp and salted like a leaf in brackish water
scuttled his feet like tacks on the rocks of Buzzards Bay.
The fish cast snow sideways from their gills.
The day bred all the far wood and death of a Territory.
We rowed mightily, blue-handed, with the heavy sway of beavers.
There was little land in sight. White rain; clouded light.

                    By noon each new snow
fired the sea like pistols in a fog. We saw the Nobska light.
For years now, its banks had been taken by the sea and pushed
farther and farther back; The smaller pines began to fall;
the rocks, bared, took the turbine of water
like grapeshot by the Hyannis Amusement Park. White rain;
the sleet began. "Remote," someone had said. We were back
in new Territory. Tonight was my first night.

                    Each year we think
the sea will freeze; each decade we forget. Red
with seaweed, blue with frosty crabs, the great sea breaks
and settles with the gently tilting boats
on Plymouth Bay. The lions swim the sea.

Dave Etter

Postcard To Florida

What brightens up this prairie town in spring?
Not tulip, not dandelion, not willow leaf,
but New Holland, Massey-Ferguson, and John Deere.
Right, the brand new farm equipment,
glistening now in the rooster-strutting sun.
And oh what colors they have given us:
strawberry-red, sweet-corn yellow, pie-apple green.
A fragrant breeze drifts in from the plowed farms.
The excitement of crops seeds my furrowed brain.
Mother, we have come through another wintertime,
and I had to write and tell you this.

Bright Mississippi

It's certainly a lead-pipe cinch pardner,
that I'm in a dark blue funk.
I can no longer root hog or die
till the cows come home to this farm.
You got to know the ropes to go against the grain,
and scratchin' around in the soil
aint exactly been my cup of Budweiser.
But I can still cut the mustard
and wont take no back seat
to some highfalutin fly-by-night dude
who dont know if he's afoot or on horseback.
I'm turnin' over a brand new leaf, you see.
I've got other fish to fry
when I get across that bright Mississippi water.
And I aint singin' you no tune
the old cow died of, neither.
Remember, pardner, you done got the real goods,
straight from the horse's mouth,
which, while no manna from heaven,
is nevertheless within an ace of the gospel.

James Fawbush

Driving Home From Park River
North Dakota in August

A winter of hot dust
Today at work
Sand in the eyes
      the teeth
      the boots
I feel like something almost dead

I am one of five men
Moving like soiled fingers
Over the grey lace
Of Dakota roads

(The woman and child are at home
Like two more blossoms on a vine
That sinks its roots into the moon)

A twelve pack
Bolted down
And shot
One by one
Out the window
Into the ditch

A hawk
Chased off or followed
By a sparrow

Forty acres of sunflowers
With their heads down

Roland Flint

At 4 A.M. In The Kitchen

For no reason I can think of
I remember my mother spraying flies
and saying, I'm killing Germans.
That was in the dining room
of what was our house till I was five,
which means it was 1938 or '39,
and that means my mother was only
33 or 34 years old when she said it—
younger than I am now.

I didn't know anything about Poland,
or Germans, or killing,
and the spray can, the old kind,
plunger, muzzle, tank,
looked like another toy to me,
a cartoon fly or bug.

Then a girl named Florence Bruce
(it comes as I write this:
she looked like my mother)
told me that in addition to Germans, flies, other people,
everyone else dies, *everyone*,
and she must have made me believe it,
because now the names "Florence" or "Bruce"
make me uneasy,
as if Florence Bruce is holding death,
the rope fraying.

I don't know what's become of Florence Bruce,
after deaths to: her brother, my sister,
friends, Poland, Germany, Hitler—
the century's-since long cemeteries of roll-call,
but my mother, whose teeth were going bad,
who had bobbed hair, and who,
it turns out, never killed anyone,
my mother whom, I realize in the kitchen this morning,
after all the years of books and pretensions,
I still love deeply,
my mother is 67 this morning, or 68 years old,
both of us almost through
and gone like a harmless spray.

Starting A Notebook At New Year's

Hello new book, new year,
I greet you down—
poems stories life.
The year has not been good.
There was stupidity, malice, jealousy,
ineptness, treachery...
some of these were not mine.

Who cares?

I do book and year a little care,
especially care for you, my book,
long and new and almost white as heroin
and I'm hooked
empty space and chance of you.

Prayer, Poor Sinners, Homely Girls

Father today I forgave that sinner myself his pain
for the homely girls hoodwinked and left,
for heavy girls crying the goodbye boy
did lay them down in small time pastures,
for the wide nosed farmers' daughters
who swung like lonely cows in town
and there were milked, stripped, and left,
again, to brood and ruminate.

Yes I forgive him Father your pain of his past
as may please God the girls
and thrive.

Carolyn Forché

Mientras Dure Vida, Sobra El Tiempo

Memory becomes very deep, weighs more, moves less.

1

She is a good woman, walking
in the body of a twisted bush, as old
as the ones who are gone.
Her teeth, chips of winter river
thawed, swallowed
or spit out.

On the way to town her hands
fly in and out her shawl
catching scraps of her voice
feathers fallen from birds.
Like mudhens, her hands.

She buys coffee, medicine, pork.
Squats on the grocery floor
digging in her breasts
for money.
She is no higher than chamisa
or wild plum trees
grown for more than a hundred years
beside the river.

2

I feel the mountains moving
closer, with smoke
on their faces, hear cries
in couloirs of snow.

Last night a woman not alive
came to my bedside, a black skirt, black
reboso. She touched
my blankets, sang like wind
in a crack, saw
that my eyes were open.
She went to the kitchen
without footsteps,
rattled pans, sang *ma-he-yo*

Ma-he-yo until morning.

3

On the way from town Rosita
leads me through rosy dust of North Plaza.
My face shrivels, I shrink through her
doorway.

On her walls, a washtub, Jesus.
One room.
La yerba del manso tied,
hung from a nail to dry.
Green chili, a blanket
dyed to match the field.
She has lived alone.

4

Rosita kneeling at her fogon,
since morning no fire.
Wind bony, dark as her face
when at night she holds
her eyes in her hands.

She stacks stumps of pinon,
lights a match.
I drop like pinon at her feet.
Fire rushes from her hands, her hands
flutter, flames, her bones
shine like tongs through her flesh.

Sparks on the ground turning into women
who begged to be let go, that night
on the llano.
People talk, people tell
these stories.
People say "leave Rosita alone or you are
malificiada."
Her laugh is a music
from the time of Christ.

Rosita's eyes shatter
la tristesa de la vida,
dog-stars within them.

You, you live alone
in your life.
Your life will have ma-he-yo.
I never married, never
cut my hair.
Ma-he-yo are blessings of God.
That is all the English I have.

5
On another day she disappeared,
her door open, her eyes
seen in the face of a dog
near the river.

You will light fires
with one touch.
You will make one death
into another.

Carol Frost

A Small Bird, Kept

She sits in her old cloth
and wants to go home
where she knows the sky
is wilder blue and ripe
with voices of her friends
who don't sit in their crumbs
of winter bread and broken
wings. Yesterday was finer
and not so cold. A gust
blows snow like scattered seeds
between the window and the sun.
"In Frankfurt where the rooms
are mine, I want to die with friends."
Only when she has pneumonia
and sleeps all day does she turn
from the light curled like a bird
and gentle in her box-bed.
Only then doesn't she whisper
to her fluttering hands
a worn, escaping song.

Gene Frumkin

Long & Shadowy Habits

Those old Jews in their shadowy habits
turned the clock morning noon and night
numbering
        the wrinkles on God's brow
numbering grains in flowing clouds
counting grass counting milk and sheep
                            possessed
      by the winding roads
that led from antiquity
                in circles in ovals
and triangles
        to the temple behind their eyes
Shadowy their habits
          Who would trust
such whiskery sophists who wisely
prepared no trust in any other tongue?
It was in figures
       of dance
food   and of myth
         these shopkeepers
dealt   pretending to count
the coins of whatever evanescent realm
they mocked by lodging in
         Bearded and seedy
sideburned and nosey
        longdead Jews
hoboes in kingdoms and duchies whose crowns are daisies
snoopers into the nuptials of Heaven and Earth
gossips of infinite configurations
  timeless keepers of the manycolored bargain

The state of New Mexico   1970
and you read the daily skies
for news
       of these ancestral spirits
They wear feathers in their long braided hair now
and somewhere in the chosen Holy Hopi Land
       their beards have finally
split   with laughter
         Their clean mugs dyed red
there they are
      still playing for
         room board and promises

Passing By

Living on high desert
where the miles are candles
in any direction   minute illuminations
as you go   barely visible
trained eye needed to mark each one
ear gifted to recollect what it was
that it was something
called out from brush and lava rock:
living on the desert
there is only the frailest scent
of trout and barracuda
sailing on the junipers
Living so
          you move with your herd
from Rio Grande to Pig River
and on to the next watering place
shaggy and dull   head so low to the Earth
you are a cloud of the buffalo

What is there to know out here
but the ghost of an earlier planet?
Its annals of light
reach you many years too late
Only the laboratories are insulated
from dust storms that bury everything else
under archeological sands
In the laboratories the water supply
is without limit and the light
never flickers
          Toward clarity
these devoted buildings sustain
their luminosity   It's good to hear them there
like white thread waltzing surely
through savage cloth
                    as we pass by

We, outside, have learned to value
innocent mountains (which, being there
obstruct our travel) as much as highways
which lead us on
the white lines the yellow lines
toward the next stop
Clear thought loves the mountains, yes
and every inarable acre

The Moon At Canyon de Chelly

Tonight the moon is limned on a slanting wall
of the White House ruin in Canyon de Chelly.
Centuries ago a different moon
bleached this same wall, perceived by the Dine
as a story to be told at dawn.

Tonight this moon is not a story.
It is a law. Still, its composition on the wall
at Canyon de Chelly recalls that private moon,
the first each of us ever saw. Though the pueblo
is dead, we hear the story its people told:

This moon drains the brown and gray,
the ochre and pink from the earth. It whitewashes
everything. That is what it does.
Now, as the sun returns to us at dawn,
we see that the moon was only pretending.

They did not say it so. It is someone among us
who, recalling some private moon, having forgotten
its name, pretends to hear its echo here.
And we all do that, call out in our own voice,
to our oldest moon, this one on the cliffside wall.

Patricia Goedicke

In The Body Shop

*"Highway death toll exceeds losses in last war by ten
percent. . . .One out of three marriages doomed to divorce. . ."*

Once I was a dream
Of Beauty:

Jewel box for holding you
Tenderly, tightly

Together we broke
Every speed limit in sight

But then came the sirens:

Bad dreams like motorcycle cops,
Bad dreams like telephone poles heading
Straight through the windshield of my face.

Now, forced to abandon the roads
Where love ambles along, on two feet

I accuse you of having invented me
For nothing but your own satisfaction:

Sprawled on the lift with my knees spread out
With the hood up and your heads inside

Do you think I don't feel you poking around down there
Trying to make my pistons purr?

Don Gordon

Mortal

They say the length of my life
Is in the nature of the veins
Of my ancestors,
Enclosed like a worm in the genes
By people I never knew.

How can I tell the age of their hearts
Who perished in a far-off village
Under a mountain of collapsing lava,
Or lay in the streets of the peninsula
In the year of the plague;
Or how long he would have lasted,
The young forebear, his brain trepanned
By a sword in the foreign war.

O great obscure manifold branches
Of the tree of the family of man,
Where does the artery begin or end
That determines the time?

Mothers, fathers, fallen in seasons
Like leaves and blown over the cold plain
Of that country, did you ever exceed
The grandfathers in their winters?

The answer is not forthcoming from them;
It is on its way with the progress
Of the multiple independently targeted re-entry vehicle
Or its next of kin.

Memorial Day

My God they're still marching
Down Main Street on Memorial Day,
Still playing John Philip Sousa
In the spirit of the year of the child.
The last bare-bones village
Offers the little flags like incense
To the burned-down image of themselves.

They have the annual heart
To put flowers on the skeletons,
To remember the legless, the eyeless,
The reasons for the last six or seven wars,
The uncounted surreptitious landings
On malarial coasts.

They don't know Pompeii is flat,
Herculaneum is finished,
The Maya have left their cities.
They don't know the whole thing
Blew down the Yalu that December.

They don't even see the fine ash
Falling on their houses
And their praying mantis heads.
They just go marching down Main Street
On Memorial Day
Like, man, two hundred years ago.

Kate Green

Letter To My Life

My life,
fine as a sliver of glass
that has somehow entered the body,

you float foreign and brilliant
in the dark flesh of the world,
tearing off tiny pieces of skin

Wherever you go, you injure the present

Daily I have watched you
come back from your homeland
to be with me
You have told me of the bells
that inhabit the place
and the streets of silence where you wander
finding yourself suddenly written
on my hand
like a scar

I have felt you
open your lips
to the future,
as thighs will sometimes
swell into bloom
the moment before touching

I have felt you turn
in the unmade bed of the day
toward that face which turns away
and I know, my life,
how you want to make love
to that silence

How I wish I could gather you whole
out of the tangled sheets
so that you could stand with me
at this window
watching the sky
combing its hair with the trees!

Alvin Greenberg

The House of the Would-Be Gardener: VI

under a single light you consider
the condition of your grapes. the radio

says to you, 'new moon wine tastes sour,
sour.' you live in an almanac

of caution, holding the fruit in your hand
just so. then the time comes to see

how things are arranged. you open the door.
over your head the moon goes up and down,

up and down, full to bursting.
at long last you cease looking for precedents

in your morality of tides and begin
to move with it, up and down, up and down,

all night long, squeezing your hands
and letting the thick, sweet juice run out.

The Sealed Room Mystery

the idea of winter in minnesota is a terrible idea.
philosophers who sit down, at night, in warm studies,
behind locked doors and windows, to fix, in their minds,
this idea of 'winter', are struck dead by it.

they fall from their chairs in their quiet studies.
they land gently on the green carpets of their studies

and are found, in the morning, by their housekeepers
—by housekeepers in buenos aires and venice and tokyo
as well as in mankato and duluth and redwing
(for philosophers, like winter, are everywhere)—

the very idea of their bodies cold and stiff,
the long green shag of their carpets suddenly white.

The Arts of the Midwest

meanwhile the waves of lake superior
imitate the pacific, beating their brains out
against some of the best granite we and our

friends have ever seen. then someone proposes
to fix, from time, this single moment,
its nature, its effect, and yes, its causes,

how it is, quite simply *so*, no comment
or moral, theme or plot or editorial,
just an amber wave, cast in cement

upon a cement shore. 'an urban sore!' we all
exclaim, disgusted as the waves that hiss
too familiarly, a bit too much more real

than a concrete lake up to our undressed
feet. still, that's *our* lake: we can't let it go
without objection! so we all line up to piss,

squatting or standing on the shore as though
it were an art to congregate like this
and with each little stream join the greater flow.

Richard Grossman

Viper

If somebody is in the way
he'd better look down or else.
I sleep all winter with my eyes and mouth open,
letting the silence filter through my body, waiting

for new opportunities. My skin
is something to behold from a distance,
which I have often done.

I have a thing about the Irish, all of whom
escaped my needle grasp.
Some say I have polluted the human race.
Some say I would like to turn their women

into salamis
in despite of their failing men

Porcupine

My natal chart
is of the bundle variety, meaning I must try
hard to relate

Everybody asks me how I make love,
but then nobody wants to try it.

Then I get angry and swing my tail
around and everybody ducks.
I don't think they take me seriously.

I've tried to tell them,
I want them to know how I try
to be decent.
I want to be respected for what I am:

a cuddly little animal,
burdened with swords.

Frog

I wrote those plantation melodies
America loves
at the first vocable point of terrestial
ancestry,

and now I sling them through the reeds
and at night
command the forests and the moon.

I remember what it was like in that other medium,
wrapped in goo,
how I used my now invisible tail to stay
a survivor. Today

I age, waiting to be hypnotized sensually
by a snake.
Once upon a time, there was a princess who magically
turned into a frog.

and lived happily ever after with her
competent lover.

Patricia Hampl

The Marsh at Boy River, Minnesota

1. The Child Pretends to Walk on the Marsh
Here our marsh is so thick and wide
we walk on it
snapping up field daisies and ground cherries
hugged close to the earth, hugged to us.
Chasing gophers and field mice until we fall,
dazed angels, face up, arms out,
letting the meadow revolve with us
with the sun with silence into sleep.

2. War
I sit at the table, this time alone.
I understand the cynical loon,
his circle, his dip, his rising
digesting a sunfish.
The marsh hides the wide river;
it rests on the river like a pale garden.
Both the loon and the sunfish knew,
but the sunfish lived there:
the loon, waiting for evidence, stalked.

3. Nostalgia at Harvest
The ricing canoes remind us
bread grows on our river.
Green and slack from the water
into these brittle old men.
From here the canoes are tiny, gliding reapers,
silent and ungreedy. They are sad
to take their rights.
From invisible waters
they gather their harvest.
The grains, greased like braves,
are brown in the canoes.
The ricers sift the narrow bodies
through their hands.

Joanne Hart

When Your Parents Grow Old
for Catherine Lupori

When your parents grow old
your mother's stories tangle
tongue and teeth in shrunken gums
Your father hears only
fading whispers of his virtue
Bloodwhistles through his brain
sing the deafness song
Like delicate whorled shells
their subtle colors
fade and grey in the
harsh winter dusk

Carefully by lamplight
you handle them
old treaties crumbing yellow edges
at your table
Deer for their lodge
driven through tangled freeways
pursued in aisles and queues
you bring them

And the change rises and sets
moves through moons until you see
your mother staring from the mirror
and you feel her breasts
her thickened waist
her thighs under your hands
and you know at last you bear and nurture them
the old ones
as you were and as
you too will be

Joy Harjo

Kansas City Coyote

Black shiny hair
like crow and
jean jacket raggy
around the edges
Like a Kansas City coyote
you are
strutting your point-toe
  boots
that you bought for
a dollar down
  around
the time so
easy   because
  a Kansas City coyote
don't fall so hard
as
  a Kansas City cowboy

Going Towards Pojoaque, A December Full Moon/72

the moon
is making silver
snail tracks
over the frozen
white earth
it is a winter ghost
hunting
for old bones
in the snow

the full moon
was so bright
i could see the bones
in my hands

Margaret Hasse

My Mother's Lullaby

Soon there will be no one
to tell me what I was like
when I was a little girl.

When my mother
smelling of milk and bread
brushes the long robe of my hair
and the vines spring roses.
We wake in a white bed,
delicious with feather pillows,
morning patterns her face.
She curls me in her arms,
she is a shell,
white and full of song.

And now I come
to tuck my little mother into bed.
I am too young to be empty-armed
and the weeds in my throat
will not let me sing lullabies.

Waiting has teeth in it.

My mother smiles at me
and wraps around herself.
I won't see her cry,
her wheat body does not even shake.
She will not know that echoes turn barbed.
Silent tears are turquoise
peacock feathers which tickle
and the hyena in me laughs,
crazy, crazy.

I do not want to adopt old ladies,
I want my own.

And my mother
on her thin shelved bed
hears the dogs move restlessly,
the clack of their nails on linoleum.
She knows they have come for her.
She whimpers, they whimper.

I will have no one who knew me
when I was a child.

Robert Hedin

Houdini

There is a river under this poem.
It flows blue and icy
And carries these lines down the page.
Somewhere beneath its surface
Lying chained to the silt
Tricky Harry holds his breath
And slowly files
His fingernails into moons.
He wonders who still waits at the dock
If the breasts of those young girls
Have developed since he sank.
He thinks of his parents
Of listening to the tumblers
In his mother's womb
Of escaping upward out of puberty
Out of the pupils in his father's eyes
And those hot Wisconsin fields.
He dreams of escaping from this poem
Of cracking the combinations
To his own body
And those warm young safes
Of every girl on the dock.
Jiggling his chains
Harry scares a carp that circles
And nibbles at his feet.
He feels the blue rush of the current
Sweeping across his body
Stripping his chains of their rust
Until each link softens
And glows like a tiny eel.
And Tricky Harry ascends.
He slips with the water through his chains
And moving upward
Climbing over and over his own air bubbles
He waves to the fish
To his chains glittering
And squirming in the silt.

He pauses to pick a bouquet
Of seaweed for the young girls on the dock.
Rising he bursts the surface of this poem.
He listens for shouts.
He hears only the night
And a buoy sloshing in the blue.

Dacotah Territory 15, Carol Smith

Roberta Hill

E UNI QUE A THE HI A THO, Father

White horses, tails high, rise from the cedar.
Smoke brings the fat crickets,
trembling breeze.
Find that holy place, a promise.
Embers glow like moon air.

I call you back from the grasses.
Wake me when sand pipers
fly. They fade,
and new sounds flutter. Cattails at sunrise.
Hair matted by sleep.

Sun on the meadow. Grey boughs lie tangled.
The ground I was born to
wants me to leave.
I've searched everywhere to tell you
my eyes are with the hazels.

Wind swells through fences, drones a flat ache for hours.
At night, music would echo
from your womanless bedroom.
Far down those bleaching cliffs,
roses shed a torrent.

Will you brush my ear? An ice bear sometimes lumbers west.
Your life still gleams, the edges melting.
I never let you know.
You showed me, how under snow and darkness,
the grasses breathe for miles.

Rory Holscher

A Beatitude

Blessed are the bewildered,
for they have listened to all the gods at once.

Mississippi Valley Slowdown

we've lived in the valley less than two hundred years
it takes longer than that for a creek bed to settle

abandoned plows and steam tractors
are smothered by wild grapes and creepers

no one has told me but i'm willing to bet
that all lock-and-dams are sliding downstream
a fin's width every ten years

they're seeing more coyotes in iowa
grey wolves have come back to wisconsin

i knew an old man who kept sharpening one knife
til he handled a blade thin as starlight

Joseph Hopkins

How I Won at The Olympic Games

When I was a scared kid
I made my First Communion
The church was packed and kneeling
My knees ached
So I held back on the last Sin
Eating meat on Friday
When Father gave me the Sacrifice
The Host stuck in my dry mouth
I couldn't swallow
His Body and Blood
Choking, I went blindly up the aisle
Until I noticed
This big pot of water at the end
That I had to pass by
I screamed, and started running
Cannibals everywhere.

Writer
Sunday: San Francisco

A traffic signal
has hung up the intersection again
just below my keyed-up typewriter
stopping in celebration
half a dozen Italian marriages
a kind of noisy menopause
each driver is calculatedly waiting
for a headless leader
who will test out general motors bumpers

While I wait hopefully
for a sherman tank to appear
on this indecisive battlefield
where the forces of the Pope
are rioting with auto horns.

Richard Hugo

Living Alone

I felt the empty cabin wasn't abandoned.
The axe, for one thing, blood still moist
on the blade. Then, warm coffee on the stove.
God, it blew outside. The owner, I said,
won't last long in this storm. By midnight
I was singing. I knew the cabin was mine.
Fifty years later, he still hadn't returned.

Moss covered the roof by then. I called
the deer by name. Alice, I liked best.
Winslow, next. Reporters came to write me up.
They called me 'animal man' in the feature
in the photogravure. The story said I led
a wonderful life out here. I said clouds
were giant toads but they quoted me wrong.

The coroner identified the bones as woman.
I denied I'd been married and the local
records backed me. Today, they are hunting all over
the world for the previous owner.
I claim the cabin by occupancy rights.
I pray each dawn. How my words climb cedars
like squirrels uttered by God.

Places and Ways to Live

Note the stump, a peach tree. We had to cut it down.
It banged the window every wind. Our garden
swayed with corn each summer. Our crops were legend
and our kindness. Whatever stranger came, we said,
'Come in.' We ran excited. 'Someone's come to see us.'
By night we were exhausted. The dark came early
in that home, came early for the last time soon.

Some nights in motels, I wake bewildered by the room.
Then I remember where I am. I turn the light on
and the girl's still there, smiling from the calendar
whatever the year. When I'm traveling, I'm hurt.
I tune in certain radio stations by heart,
the ones that play old tunes like nothing worthwhile's
happened since that funeral in 1949.

When I'm in the house I've bought, I don't dwell on
the loss of trees, don't cry when neighbors move away
or dogs get killed by cars. I'm old enough to know
a small girl's tears are fated to return, years from now
in some Berlin hotel, though I seem to sit unfeeling
at the window watching it all like a patron.
I'm taking it in, deep where I hope it will bloom.

That is the crude self I've come to. The man who says
suffer, stay poor and I can create. Believe me, friends,
I offer you your homes and wish you well in them.
May kisses rain. May you find warm arms each morning.
May your favorite tree be blooming in December.
And may you never be dispossessed, forced to wander
a world the color of salt with no young music in it.

David Ignatow

The trees across the road are stalking
the house that has displaced their ancestors.
The house has nowhere else to go
and stays where it is, afraid
of the lightning that trees attract
in a storm.

———————————————————

It's snowing, I want to hear a human voice
over the phone talking animatedly
about things we hold in common.
I think the snow is going to bury us.

Dale Jacobson

The Child Running Toward His Death

In fast panic his feet
beat against the ground,
the heavy feet of the child
running toward his death.

As he runs he stares
with sudden eyes into earth;
his blood knows how to lose
and wants to pull him down.

His hand grasps at the air.
"Hold me!" he cries
as the air slips through his fingers.
"Hold me!" as his wild hair
leaps into the wind.

Our Hands

Nothing comes to our hands
that is not already touched
with the savage rage of having left—

small utensils and loves,
paper, pens, even our fingernails
that protect us against being torn
are each one called
to their tiny destructions.

These minutes collect and fall
like ages from the tips of branches—
the white of an apple opened to the sun,
distance flowing out from the core!

Dan Jaffe

Poem For a Bar Mitzva

My son has dreamed me dead
all over my right
to do with his life
what wisdom wills.
He'd bop my dictates with a Louisville slugger,
yank my level of diction down to asphalt,
stick a barb under my theoretical discourse.
He won't be fooled by language or logic
& he won't buy a soft sell from a hard old man.

He'll damn well climb his own shakey ladders,
fling bottles from garage roofs,
streak into the forbidden darkness
while my advice hardly stains his jeans.
Me, the rabbi, his grandfathers,
he's stuck us all limply in a vase
to gently wither out our days.
But Pop he says, you're imagining it all;
I never said what you said I said,
and here we are again
trying to cage facts with feelings.

Yesterday, the air conditioner broken,
I yelled, Get back here, to a pair of deaf sneakers.
He ran like a tormented fox,
leaving me to sweat it out without a script,
to sulk in my Director's chair.

He explained to us later,
hugged us, said we were silly to worry,
brushed his teeth before bed.

He's on his way to his own sins,
so says the Law. It's about time:
My bingo boards loaded with his numbers.
But my father just smirks. How he loves
the younger generation he's free from.

I Have No Way With Gardens

I have no way with gardens,
Weeds spring from my lightest footsteps,
Seed the wind with flags of distress.
But once I knew a girl golden as wheat,
Her smiles, promises ripening to harvest,
A singular flower who seemed all bloom.

That season's gone. But before
We are pulped and packed, our tendrils withered,
Before the years close like the covers of an album,
I would win back more than a toast,
A reminder of easier wonders,
More than a flagon of dust from a weed choked well.
But a clear draught in a landscape of love.

For Langston Hughes

You slung your poems over your shoulder
And bobtailed off, while the rubbed coins swirled
Through the subway slot. We rushed after,
Called from the platform. Too late!
One palm slightly raised, you wavered
Down the shuddering aisle. You became a blur
Adrift in a thousand tilting rooms.
No one had time to say goodbye.

We kept on, chewing our chicken,
Picking our teeth, even as we flinched,
Feeling the neon sharpen through the glass,
The shadows heavy on our bones.
But somewhere behind the counter
Your laugh flickers. On a broken cup
You tap out a beat to make us dance.

John Judson

Master Charge

Why buy a tied bow
instead of tying one
except to promote the irony
of economy
that kills to make us secure,
that makes us wonder
about the thin men around
the world's corner
in whose faces we read lines
like those in our son's.

Merry Christmas, birds!
You now have a new house
made of redwood
and seeds at K-Mart's cost,
with the addition of 18%
we carry as a charge.

It is a guilt we pay for
that god is not the president,
as we continue to reach
for his wallet, to which
unlike the ripe apples
of the first tree's wonder,
we keep ourselves chained.

Deborah Keenan

A Poem About White Flowers

my father chose a train
gave it the gift of his body
bright july sun
the engine lifted his form
hurled it   scattered it   moved on
we pretended there was enough left
to cremate

and the white flowers you gave me are so right
they fill my home   i think of them
slashes of petal white
i play endless game after endless loss
of solitaire
just so i can sit with those slashing white flowers
i love these flowers from you
they surprise me the way the roses didn't
they touched me the way a good white cliche
is supposed to touch all women who believe
in words like white and fragrance   who believe
in daises pretending to be zinnias and in daisies
swearing they are white chrysanthemums

by the tracks my brother searched
for father's property
july sun burning to nothing the last
fragments of my father's beautiful
piano hands
he found the wallet   torn pictures
pieces of identity that identified
a man who came to dread his own

by the train station my brother found
two lovers who had been giving each other
their bodies
when they heard the train's emergency scream
when they heard they forgot the pleasure
they had been seeking and sought another
when they looked up the air carried
my father toward them   they were frightened
by the blood   the choice of death
so near their open fields of love

and the white flowers you gave me
don't fade today   the white
phosphorescent against a winter gray window
i love them for not fading today
for being white   not red   not dying   not red
for being white   and themselves
whatever they are   whatever they become

Dacotah Territory 13, Linda Hanson

Stanley Kiesel

Lines On No One

What are *you* doing in my parish?
Here, we are all sitting ducks
Living off our undernourished
Sinecures. Each one of our desires
Ends in petty thievery
Or illegal entry. What retires
Long before retirement age
Is reality. But hope works on,
Like a drayhorse, pulling you
On its rope, deeper into the provinces
Of Never Never Land, where those
In heat wait to inherit
Anything they can come across.
Who could guess we'd meet?
Who would dream we would spring
From a deck of cards
To be the knaves of hearts?
But the pretender is no less
A personage. It is the memory
Of the knave we shall take into
Old age, not the rightful heir;
The rights of succession bore us.
And rightly so. What is more
Exciting than dispossession? Than
The transgressor. He fills history.
Is history. —Come, and I'll tell
You a story about the land of
Innuendo where there is nothing
To be seen for miles
But inklings glowing in the sand.
A scene laid to attract
The nearly impossible.
Fingermarks on an old theme,
Yes, but what else is there
Between the iron parenthesis?
Why else bare this shameless
Penmanship? Consent. Simply that.
Your unmitigated consent to this
Generative limb which seeds
Whatever yields to it.

William Kloefkorn

Haywire Cox

This small song for Haywire Cox,
his limbs at rest at last now
at the bottom of our beermugs.

Haywire Cox, kicked in the head
by a milkcow no more dangerous,
Stocker said,
than a Baptist neutered.

What Haywire Cox was doing behind that cow,
and at such an angle,
only Haywire's arms and hands
and fingers ever knew—
and try as they might,
they were never able to flail forth the truth.
Like wires busted on a bale of hay,
Stocker said,
holding nothing and going off
dead-ended in all the wrong directions.

Yet their tireless antics said it all:
there had to be a reason,
and a good one,
sure as Adam broke his teeth on apples.
And he who doubts it, Stocker said,
does so at his own and everlasting peril.

Thus this small song for Haywire Cox,
his animation at rest at last now
at the bottom of our beermugs.

And a toast,
Stocker says,
to that one fountain, cow or Christ,
whose will commands the awful imprint
that knows best.

Some Day This Will Happen To Us Too

Without notice
the new girl appears in the classroom,
filling the desk that Loren Barker
slipped away from.
Behind her dark eyes
moil the mismatched twins,
hope and horror.

By recess she has eaten
all of one pencil
and half of another.
A porcupine of slivers
bubbles the blood
on her lower lip.

Some day this will happen
to us too.
We will hear first
a shuffling of pots and pans
in the kitchen,
then voices one note huskier
than most times call for.

Once on the road, we will stop
only for relief and sandwiches.
Somewhere between here and there
something like salt
from a nearby lick
will form on the tongue.
Now children, hear me:
when it happens
it will be too late.
We will be already there,
or very nearly,
and dead, at the very least,
or, at the very most, alive and young.

John Knoepfle

why are you here
black bones

I talked too much
white bones

why are you here
white bones

black bones
don't you know why

_____

spoiled meat and starvation
and agents who cheated them
drove the santee off their
reservations and they had their
several triumphs until
the militia crushed them
and the corpse of little crow
dumped in a garbage heap
was found and stretched out and flayed

they had it all
the complete victory
and the land too
gutted and cut up for homesteads

they had it all
the barb on a hook
even this poem

Ted Kooser

Shooting A Farmhouse

The first few wounds are nearly invisible;
a truck rumbles past in the dust
and a .22 hole appears in the mailbox
like a fly landing there.
In a month you can see sky
through the tail of the windmill.
The attic windows grow black and uneasy.
When the last hen is found shot in the yard,
the old man and his wife move away.

In November, a Land-Rover
flattens the gate like a tank
and pulls up in the yard. Hunters spill out
and throw down their pheasants like hats.
They blow out the rest of the windows,
set beercans up on the porch-rails
and shoot from the hip.
One of them walks up and yells in,
"Is anyone home?" getting a laugh.

By sunset, they've kicked down the door.
In the soft blush of light,
they blast holes in the plaster
and piss on the floors.

When the beer and the shells are all gone,
they drive sadly away,
the blare of their radio fading.
A breeze sighs in the shelterbelt.
Back in the house,
the newspapers left over from packing
the old woman's dishes
begin to blow back and forth through the rooms.

Walking To Work

Today, it's the obsidian
ice on the sidewalk
with its milk-white bubbles
popping under my shoes
that pleases me, and upon it
a lump of old snow
with a trail like a comet
that somebody,
probably falling in love,
has kicked
all the way to the corner.

A Hairnet With Stars

I ate at the counter.
The waitress was wearing
a hairnet with stars,
pale blue stars
over the white clouds
of her hair, a woman
still lovely at sixty
or older, full-breasted
and proud, her hands
strong and sensual,
smoothing the apron
over her belly.
I sighed and she turned
to me smiling.
"Mustard?" she asked.

Miriam Levine

Working: The Egg Keeper

Riding the fork lift
down long waxed corridors
in shatterproof glasses
iron toed safety shoes
moving blue plastic
past the blinking console
monitoring moon rockets
blue and green raised maps
where continents wrinkle and furrow
the heart and lung machine
a constant electric whine
inside the refrigerator
lights on
blue, infra-red, neon
shining on the eggs
you stack
thin white blue-veined
neat and cold in rows—
the heavy enamel doors close—
zipping up your back packer's jacket
thin as parachute silk, cerise
pink like a flare in the snow.

Daniel Lusk

Understudy

Old men who eat alone in small cafes
arrange the silver carefully
beside the plate.

It crawls inside their cuffs
and edges out again along their temples
and the gothic arches of their brows.

Arranging is the life
now
isn't it.

Old men check their watches
frequently,
lest the sand run out unnoticed
onto the table by the water glass.

Their hands flutter
over the fork and spoon again, the knife,
as if the knife were a lost opportunity
or a love
that might be set to rights.

Attentive as they are to these
small handles,
I suspect if they let go

they'll belly up with loneliness
and float off toward the ceiling fans
in all these small cafes

where I sit watching, hours on end,
to learn their little order,
eating alone.

Richard Lyons

Of Robert Lowell

It was always trying to get out,
Trying to become.
Being trapped in flesh,
It battered against your teeth a while,
Intense, compressed, furious,
Sounding like singing,
Until you stopped to catch your breath.
The you of you, inside its habitation,
Perceived that violence would get it nothing
and relaxed,
Knocked on the windows of your mind
With a soft fist, deceiving us all
Beautifully,
But always, always
       trying to get out.
Your skull refused, a close enclosure.
It kicked your head at times,
Drumming like poetry
To be released.
It drew lines of battle with you
Which you scanned, sadly.
Pain was its message to you, well,
That it pounded into poems
And broken love.
That you of you persisted,
Angry and still, waiting,
Watching, in the red dark
Found your heart,
Softer than your mind.
And squeezed
Until your heart let go.

Restricted Love

On my sixteenth birthday
I was given a beautiful knife.
I learned soon to carve
my initials in my desires.
I claimed the ash tree
and our garage and the door
of my own room, with the date.

My pride of possession grew,
I loved what I could carve.

But there are limits, I suppose.
I have never loved the air,
and I tried only once
to love a woman.

The Fan Dancer

Gypsy Rose it's called,
"the biggest stripper in the West."
She scoops aside her grass fan
to bare the luring layers
of black rock that make men come
running in fantasies of profitable love.
Will they, in the morning,
wake to the cold gray
of spent energies and hungers
on the hard bed rock
of a ravaged life,
the grass gone,
the stripper gone,
the dream gone,
the dust on the window,
the dry wind blowing?

Chicago

Look at the moving hands,
the moving arms
like weeds in the wind,
like wind scattering a ragweed fever
over the American-desert
livingrooms
in the house of the world,
the whole world watching,
watching the picture,
the glass of running color,
the glass streaked like a mouth,
a mouth in agony
in a Francis Bacon painting.

The solid sound of wooden law
rings on the hard heads,
on the hard kidneys,
on warding hands broken
like cameras.

The whole world watches
from its open boat
floating in the rage
and water of angry fear
and frozen passion.
The whole world floats
in the little oblong box
like a body,
an empty carcass
floating on a dead sea.

The clubs come down on the water.

David Martinson

In Praise Of Neglected Ladders

What use are ladders pointing in the air?
Those aimed at windows are covered with gauze
The ones in the orchard soon sprout leaves and
Disappear in a burl of apple boughs,
And always climbing starts with heavy steps.

But fallen ladders, forgotten in weeds,
These deserve a host of benedictions,
The way the rungs connect nine inch acres
Of wild oats in morained constellations,
Beautiful are these woodpecker windows.

For they align the windmill with the barn.
Visited all hours by westerly wind,
Wheat, omphallic waters; cloud marauders,
They beckon the Pleiades with their limbs.
Ladders. I praise them even as wishbones.

And the builders of ladders! what slivers
They carry wherever they go. Below
Their skin a climbing germ festers and burns
Neglected, neglected to be found now
Sweeping, caressing the heart like a broom.

Oh workers bound together, believe me:
To broken ladders healing in the grass
All crickets, fieldmice, moles and wrens return.
Sleeping in our steps, bittersweet and ash,
All ladders traveling the last road home.

Thomas McGrath

Totems(V)

It is the special kind of night that Alvaro likes. It's not—
Or not merely—the full moon in this water-spill somewhere
In Venice L.A. It's a—kind of—let's call it a configuration:
Moon.
      Water.
          Night.
              The deep heart of the singer:
A guitar has sunk in 6 fathoms of honey. . .
                    And remember:
The secret oils of Venice have transformed the transforming moon. . .

Anyway: the moon in the water. And this lunatic frog—
It *can't* be anyone but Alvaro Cardona-Hine at his old stunt:
Singing.
      He would like to have the moon, perhaps, the scabrous
Changing filth and flirt of the air-less black acres of
Night space or prisoner here in there back and blasted lots. . .
And he sings.
      The moss grows over him.
           He does not care.
           It is his

Art.
   Hu-m-m-m-m-m-m-m
           hu-m-m-m-m-m
                hu-m-m-m-m-m

Nor does the moon care, falling into the west
Like a drunken mother into an oven, her face beginning to
Char in the changing light—and all the oils and acids of
Sinister Venice cannot preserve her.
          It is then that Alvaro
Changes into a fox-squirrel and leaps to the limb of a tree!
The moon is a floating nut, the last one he needs for winter,
And he begins to coax it home in his soothing voice
With an occasional bark to let it be known who's boss.

This stimulates blasphemy and early TV among the more human
Neighbors.

After what seems like a long time, if you are a
Squirrel-singer, the moonnut dissolves in the acid pool
Or sinks to the bottom.
              Dawn, like a drunken ship, staggers
Into port at San Pedro, hoarse-horn-mourning for all of us dead at sea.

It has been a prosperous night for our poet.
                         He stuffs the fox gear
Into the back of a station wagon near Shotwell's greenhouse.
Then, forgetting they are aerodynamic anomalies that cannot fly,
(And that *he* cannot fly)he changes into a bumblebee. He has remembered.
Where, past a cut in the hills, lies a solid mile of clover.
He cannot wait for a moment—there is always too much to be done.
Humming a little—tuning the void—he is on his way
To serenade a 90 acre field of disordered and premature honey.
It will keep him busy a while: sounding many disguises. . .

There will always be time for the necessary transformations.

Giuffre's Nightmusic

There is moonrise under your fingernail—
Light broken from a black stick
Where your hands in darkness are sorting the probables.

Hunger condenses midnight on the tongue. . .
Journeys. . .Blues. . .ladder of slow bells,
Toward the cold hour of lunar prophecy:

A scale-model city, unlighted, in a shelf
In the knee of the Madonna; a barbwire fence
Strummed by the wind: dream-singing emblems.

      —The flags that fly above the breakfast food
        Are not your colors.
                    The republic of the moon
        Gives no sleepy medals. Nor loud ornament.

From A Long Way From Pah-Gotzin-Kay

With all those I love
Shining
In radiant light
At the other side of the world,
I lie down in this
Darkness.
I straighten my legs.
I close my eyes.
I try to dream of my own waking.
I hold myself in my own arms like a dead friend.

In Early Autumn

On a day when the trees are releasing the cured gold of the sun
Like the planed shavings of their own circular hearts—
Auriferous anthracite and river of exhausted butterflies;

A day, too, when the sizzling flies are fingering their rosaries of blood
In the furry cathedrals of spent flesh—artifacts—
Gone-green goners of the golden summer;

Then I know a place with three dead dogs and two dead deer in one ditch.

I feel the displacement of minerals,
The stone-grown fossils,
Under this hill of bones that calls my flesh its home.

William Meissner

Salvage

I thought I had stopped, but I hear
breath filling my mouth with that same hiss.
My lungs are flabby tires that billow with air
ten times each minute, my worn tongue floats on oil.
I would turn another corner, turn corner after
corner until my body turns
square.

Just look at me, my junkyard: metal teeth
that sharpen with rust behind the
dent of my mouth, eyes that hide beneath
the clay cliff of my forehead,
the cliff where I watch used thoughts
driving off one by one
like old cars.

Colors

"October's breath. The sun was gone,
now it puts its lips on the horizon.
The morning sky changes color
like a dark blue balloon inflating.
So tell me a story of the thin moon of ice
that floats on top of the puddle
like the water's dream. Tell me
about the lake in the corn field,
the way its center melts at mid-day
and eats the bright blue from the sky.
Tell me of the ears of corn
inside the tin silo
that know each day when the sun is rising:
ten million yellow teeth, smiling."

W.S. Merwin

To The Hand

What the eye sees is a dream of sight
what it wakes to
is a dream of sight

and in the dream
for every real lock
there is only one real key
and it's in some other dream
now invisible

it's the key to the one real door
it opens the water and the sky both at once
it's already in the downward river
with my hand on it
my real hand

and I am saying to the hand
turn

open the river

Ralph J. Mills, Jr.

The Moon

For Denise Levertov

East of Phoenix, driving into
the mountains' kneeling shadow
while a wind blows purple night
over the ridges.

the moon rises, wheel
of phosphorus,
dream of creation from
the clouds' spume
falling away.

A cool light runs ahead of me
on the road's black tongue
all the way back.

Across The Cold

For Arthur Heiserman, 1929-1975

Flakes drift on the window ledge,
then whirl off—
clouds of spiral nebulae.

The hospital's humming around
a well of silence, the exhaustion
of grief left behind.

A head whitened with snow turns away
beyond the glass;
your hands, your coat are snow too.

And your strange pitched laughter,
startling as a bird cry
across the cold we're breathing.

Howard Mohr

Ralph Nader Visits My House

Coming home late one night I find him
under the kitchen sink with a flashlight
taking down the names of canned goods.
I know it's him.
He shines the light in my face.
He reads from his list:
"Artificial colors, bulging tops,
barbituates and chemical garbage.
And this is only a beginning.
Sit down please."
I sit down, shielding my eyes,
trying to make out his face.
"Crawling between your walls
I discovered mice nested among wires.
The water heater has no safety valve.
Your attic is ticking."
"But," I say.
He smiles. "The fully documented account
of the 87 accidents you will have
is to be published in Friday's *New York Times.*"
The chair collapses when I stand,
light bulbs pop out of their sockets,
my shoe laces burst into flames.
"Your wife is also defective," he sneers,
climbing out the window
avoiding my dangerous doors.

James Moore

Death-House
for Carla Neal

1

When you blow,
wind from the other world,
when you call,
I just *may* not come.
I know my friend went
and it was wonderful, her ritual:
the candles, the ointment, the way she lay on the couch to die.
She saw how the wind moves through the little Chinese house,
a mobile in the shape of a cuckoo clock:
what a strange clock death is
when wind moves the hands,
when the figures who come out on the hour are stiff,
though arm in arm.

This dream begins awake, in daylight.
I gave Carla the little house.
I thought it was for her twelfth birthday,
but maybe it was to mark her death moving one year closer.
Later, after her dance recital, Carla told me why she cried:
"I do that all the time.
When I come out and I'm stiff
what I have to do is laugh on the inside, crack up;
but on the outside I'm sad. Then I can dance."

2

The other morning, early, even before the first shift at the Ford
plant,
I saw an old man in a suit walk by. He was hunchbacked
and carried a black bag. Maybe he was an old doctor retired,
out for a walk with his medicine. Maybe it's lonely later on.

Forgive me, those of you who must die.
I am not myself. It's like last halloween
when I wore the silver mask, the bloodless face
of something not quite human, of someone
ageless, scarey, laughable.
After the party I buried that mask under the kitchen sink.
Emma Jean, I'm sorry you saw the wind shake the house,
that you lay down to die.
But this isn't third grade any more.
I only called you names that one time.
Now, from behind this mask—
neither black nor white, male nor female—
I throw off that little death I caused you then
and the many other times for which I've been secretly ashamed all
these years.

Now we've all grown up and are on our own,
those of us who choose to live, those of us who chose to die.
For me, the death house is no longer a death house,
but not what it was before the dream either;
not just a toy I gave a little girl I love.
Like the mask thrown under the kitchen sink,
this house into which I now carry my own spirit over the threshold
was born miraculously ancient, beyond any naming as gift, dream, life or
death.

Michael Moos

The Archer

I draw the bow,
after leaving it for years,
unstrung, hanging on a wall;
I draw nock and feather
all the way back to the ear
and hold. . . And again
it is the first time, my father
showing me how to stand—
feet apart, shoulders square,
heart turned away from the target.
He gives me an arrow,
and the pig skin grip dampens
in my hand. He tells me
to forget the bull's eye
and with both eyes open, release.
My fingers are weak,
the waxed string burns my arm
and the shaft falls short.
The day fades and I grow some
in my sleep. When I wake
he's gone—so I spend the morning
bending the limbs, failing
each time, to drop the served loop
over the tip. Many times
he returns with weeks of beard,
red stains on the knife. And in time
I'm ready to wait at the edge
of a clearing at dusk, where deer trails
funnel through tall grass
into the open, into high wind.
I rise to my knees, wanting
the doe's blood. I rehearse the story
but never connect. And one year
I stop dreaming of opening her lungs,
stop living to hoist the carcass
from a rafter with a rope.
I begin hunting something else,
not knowing I would come back,
when my father could no longer return,
to draw a man, a weapon, a life
into one weight... after wanting so long
to give the arrow its freedom, I do.

Antony Oldknow

Baptism in Kansas

Jehovah went down by Jordan, Kansas,
in his old gray prayerbook hat and butterfly
moustache, to see how it was in Sodom.
He found the elders waiting in a circle
praying round a tub full of water, he saw
a white-robed girl with eyes downcast
step pious into the cold water, he saw
the split image of Himself grab her by the
shoulders and plunge her in
unresisting, while the elders in gray suits
sang a stately hymn and looked on lusting.

The dogs stood still, a horse cocked his eye
below the barn, the wind pump stopped,
a cloud hovered in the sky below which
two birds flew. This, thought the Lord,
should surely have been Eve—poor souls
(and he scratched a horn under his hat)
to have swallowed only one kind of apple
when I made all kinds. Come on he called,
seeing a rattlesnake peer from behind
the wheels of a Model T—a fang grinned
beneath the butterfly as he swept
the snake up into his jacket pocket,
touched his hat to the somber spinster in black,
twinkled blue sky at her flypaper drawers,
hopped into his chariot of fire and took off.

from John Steuart Curry's painting
of the same name (1928)

Simon Ortiz

The Creation: According To Coyote

"First of all, it's all true."
Coyote, he says this, this way,
humble yourself, motioning and meaning
what he says.

You were born when you came
from that body, the earth;
your black head burst from granite,
the ashes cooling

until it began to rain.
It turned muddy,
and then green and brown things
came without legs.

They looked strange.
Everything was strange.
There was nothing to know then,

until later, Coyote told me this,
and he was bullshitting probably,
two sons were born,
Uyuyayeh and Masawe;

they were young then
and then later on they were older;

and then the people were wondering
what was above.
They had heard rumors.

But, you know, Coyote,
he was mainly bragging,
when he said (I think),
"My brothers, the Twins then said,
'Let's lead these poor creatures
and save them,' "

and later on, they came to light
after many exciting
and colorful and tragic things
having to do with adventure,
and this is the life, all these, all these.

My uncle told me all this, that time.
Coyote told me too, but you know
how he is, always talking to the gods,
the mountains, the stone all around.

And you know, I believe him.

Joe Paddock

Eating Wild Food

salads of cattail
dandelion and plantain

and for a boiled and buttered green
give me milkweed:
stalk, pod, flower, and top leaves

bluegills and berries, catfish
broiled in long slabs

and come the fall
venison and roast raccoon

we thrive
there is nothing but teeth
in our smiles

Mary Pryor

Weasel

Born from the ear of his mother,
small as a grasshopper:

we made him a bed of thistledown in a thimble,
fed him on clover nectar and strawberry seed
crushed in a diamond mortar. The size of a mouse,
he liked to doze in pockets and ride on shoulders.

The day we found the spaniel dead on the hearthrug,
a neat incision over the jugular,
we held a family council, turned him out.

Missing him rather,
we were noncommittal when neighborhood cats disappeared,
then a Great Dane, then a pony.

Rumors fly . . .
of a huge entity raiding peripheral farms
for livestock—and not adverse to man.

(See T.H. White. The Bestiary. N.Y., 1960. p. 92)

David Ray

The Father of the Curious Child

"Did Jesus have a sense of humor?"
the kid asks on Sunday morning.
"Yes, indeed," I say, absolutely certain.
"How do you know?" she rejoins.
"I read about it," I say,
hoping to settle the question.
"Where?" she insists.
"In German," I say, imagining him laughing
robustly as he chased the moneychangers
out, giggling as he told the woman
taken in adultery to depart.
"Has it been translated?" she asks.
"I'm not sure," I say.
"In English?" she asks, "Or maybe
in Spanish. I could make it out
with a lot of time and a dictionary."
I'm back to the comics.
"Just give me an example of his sense
of humor," she says.
"He had trouble keeping from laughing,"
I say. "How do you know?" she says.
"I feel quite certain of it," I say.
At last she fades away with humming
and hawing and I feel a certain victory
as she gets back to painting a ship,
though suddenly she turns back:
"Is that the one that Bach wrote,
the little fugue in G. Major?"
"I think so," I say, loving Blondie.
"That's my favorite," she tells me,
"the little fugue in something minor."
And then she confesses, "You know, Dad,
I don't know the difference between
Major and Minor." "That's all right,"
I tell her. "When you're my age,
you will for sure." That's love,
major to minor, minor to major...
and to know the difference.

John Calvin Rezmerski

Tarzan

Lord Greystoke caught the 4:15 elephant
home from the counting house at Opar,
after a short workout
with his daily crocodile.
At the corner of Branch and Vine
he paid exact fare (peanuts in those days),
took a deep breath of monkey-smelling air,
went up to his high-rise treehouse,
found a coconut of martinis,
had one, had another,
changed into his casual loincloth,
read the paper, asked Jane,
"What's for dinner?"
She'd lost her poultry scissors, so
they'd have to go out,
in the Village.
Dinner out for a change, maybe dancing.
Off they go to the Congo Club.
Had to sit next to a bunch of, you know,
"Knee-grows."

"This world's going to hell, by Jesus,
next thing you know, they'll be moving in
right out into the treetops,
right nextdoor.
There ought to be a law of the jungle.
I know what I'm going to do," he told Jane,
"Get me a big lion, yessir,
keep it right out front.
Put up a scarecrow, too, show these
superstitious jigaboos
not to get ideas. .
One of them bucks ever lays a hand on you, Jane, he'll
have to
answer
to Tarzan.
Personally.

a-a-a-aa-aa-aa-ee-ee-ee-aa-aa-aa-ough!
King of the Apes, Lord of the Jungle!
And don't you forget it.
Me Tarzan, you waiter—
bring me another drink, Sambo,
I feel powerful thirsty, boy,
powerful."

And everybody in the place
was
staring at him
because he was
half-naked, you know,
and spoke
with a God-awful
gorilla accent.

Manifesto

If I am among the lost
count me among the horses,
not cowboys or Indians.
If you tell me to get my gun
I do not speak English.
If you see me in feathers
I am from a different tribe.
I will not take my turn
above the grass
trying to get under it.

Your Hands

Your letter came this morning
and reminded me of your hands.
The letters were like flowers
in front of a wrought-iron fence,
and wanting to pick them
reminded me of your hands.
There were no thorns in the flowers,
but there could have been,
and if I had picked them,
I could have had to pick
thorns out of my fingers,
and that reminded me of taking
the splinter out of your hand.
It's always hard
to take splinters out of your own hands,
or thorns either.
With only one hand to work with
you wind up digging
too deep and leaving a little scar.
Your hands are full of little scars.
I could feel them when you
touched me, even through
the sleeve of my jacket.
I remember that is how
you touched me
when you didn't know me,
but you could see
I was ill at ease with
no one touching me.
Your hand said kinder things
than your voice could.
Later, your voice confided
it feels like your hands
are man's hands. And if
they were, that wouldn't be so bad—
hands are only as good
as whoever lives in them,
and a man's hands would be lucky
to have a woman living in them.
As I am lucky to have lived
in your hands for a while.

George Roberts

Thanking My Father For Reading To Me
"I wish the boy were here...."
Santiago said aloud.
-Hemingway, The Old Man and the Sea

1
a famous man stands at his desk
writing a story

the thick line hanging down into the water
is a voice

a boy lifts his paper lamp   lit with oil from his father's hands
and slowly scours the night inside the sea

from its silent chamber   a blue marlin
charmed by the lamp's small flame   swims up
to taste the voice

       i begin to dream of my father now
       his hands full of torn pages

       so long has it been since he spilled
       into my sleep

       surely some kind of death has taken place

2
it is the great fish
it is the old man's hands   cut and bleeding
    by the line that holds him   to the fish
it is the boy's tears   as he watches the old man sleep
    a pot of coffee cooling between them

3

and today i begin to read the old man's story
to my son

a gloss of ocean birds   like a memory
with no place to land   rises off the page

andrew curls his fingers
around the imagined line
learning the icy sting
of the cut

and i am back on my father's lap
the *life* magazine quilting our legs

> his voice is a lamp
> that never showed him the sea

> but the air around us fills with gulls
> and waves break against the chair

4

we wake with dried salt
turning our hands silver
in the moon's light

we each drop our line into dark water
and imagine a great fish thinking about the surface

we whisper words that turn into black string
and wait for the fluted brush of fingers
the softest tug   that tells us

we have hooked a beautiful marlin
it is our son

and we must learn
by cutting our hands
how to keep him

how to let him go.

Ruth Roston

Children's Theatre

Todd on my lap.
We squirm, are frightened
inside the belly of the whale.
Nanny, is it real?

Only this morning
we rehearsed the plot
could tell each other
who was Lampwick
who was Fox and why
Pinnocchio's nose.
                            It grows now
incredibly before our eyes.
Nanny, is it real?

All the swift right answers fade.
Esse est percipii est nonsense
est irrelevant
inside the belly of the whale.

Noses long as broomsticks
branch out in leaves.
Birds sing in trees
where no trees grow.
Keep both eyes closed!
One splinter from the Snow Queen's
mirror and the Prince will drown
before your eyes.
My hands are cold, cold as the sea.
My hands are old. The coachman lies.
Nanny, is the coachman real?
We are blown clear out of our chair
when the great whale sneezes,
blown up the aisle, down steps
into October, Sunday. Our hands,
still tingling with their clapping,
scoop up leaves.

Robert Schuler

Old Testament
for Linda and Peder Hamm

lovers of children   myth-bound
to earth   the only heaven
the Sioux hated them   "bad talkers"
my German fathers who chewed their language
like thick sausage & conquered this black land
far from Eden   high west of the sea gap

tribal elder carved silver in his dark chair
Grandpa struck us with fists of a God
who told him in guttural mumbles
thunder-gristled hail stones
our thin souls were nailed to sin-shot oxmeat
we would become starved ears of *"weizen"*

he hated me   named me Adam's ass *"regenmeister"*
fooldeaf to Luther's & the Lord's commands
to shed devilflesh in humble worksweat
I drifted long afternoons of cool rain
crystal ebony sheen of crows on fences
salt & must spraying from mudflesh
wind-changed shades of green
sun-shatter in leaved water
fresh spiralling worlds

seeking roots   another generation
I taste the sweet rain of new words
as they spill loose   spin
englished through my body
to grasp & kiss seeds & skin
nerve to the holy belly of this soil
who souls my children now
starred heads of wheat
my *"sonnenkinder"*
laughing in the last paradise

Paul Shuttleworth

Mow

1

He piled the black chair
on top of a crate of picture
albums. The benediction of
a fallen house: blue velvet
flames, the bowels of a
pale calf, the click of a
fingernail on driftwood.

2

His breath in his daughter's
hair as he carries her to
bed: baked apples on a
bare wooden table. She
recalls sundown on a lake,
a crisp piece of bread.

3

He was typing when she asked
for a goodnight kiss: the
snow between two bear cubs,
a door dragged to a clearing
in the woods and set on fire.

4

Her toy blocks hold the
night. A windshield...
no, a church window pulls
into view. A full length
likeness of St. Malachy:
holy water on the naked
leg of an Irish orphan,
the winter sun through
St. Malachy's voice, a
clock as slow as a nun's
eyelid. Now a windshield
to wipe off in the rain.

Gary Snyder

Manzanita

Before dawn the coyotes
    weave medicine songs
    dream nets—spirit baskets—
    milky way music
       they cook young girls with
       to be women;
    or the whirling dance of
    striped boys—

At moon-set the pines are gold-purple
Just before sunrise.

The dog hastens into the undergrowth
Comes back panting
Huge, on the small dry flowers.

A woodpecker
Drums and echoes
Across the still meadow

One man draws, and releases   an arrow
Humming, flat,
Missing a gray stump, and splitting
A smooth red twisty manzanita bough.

Manzanita   the tips in fruit,
Clusters of hard green berries
The longer you look
The bigger they seem,

      "little apples"

David Solheim

Containers

I'd like to write poems
Like two dollar pots,
Sell them at summer sales
And make people happy,
Because my poems hold water.

Breaking Up

After she left him there, he sat,
Breathing deep, the engine running.
When he began remembering,
He said that he was glad they found
Him and brought him here to help
The others who needed his strength,
But he was ready to go home
And live.

                He told us how he went
Fishing with a friend and caught
A fish that was his wife. He hooked
Her deep and pulled her insides out.
He stayed three weeks before he cried.
He said he was not God and would
Kill himself and her, if he could.

William Stafford

A Local Statement

After their trance all night the trees
climb back into themselves again,
and though we've shut the wind out hundreds
of times, he's back, banging a stick
on the hedge, calling his leaf-footed dogs.

Sometimes there seems no outside for rooms,
that we've broken adrift and are silently
falling endlessly onward with nothing
behind us or coming and only a thread
unreeling back there thinner and thinner.

I reach for a sound and hook the great cable—
the whole world hooks on and comes to: we swing
again, saved by what's near. And only
our fears go wandering onward out there,
touching by turns through the hours all the
        miles toward the stars.

Waking in the Midwest

Some sound the trees hear
tunes their throats:
grass, mushrooms, leaves,
all report ready.
Day begins, pressed through
accepting miles
over the prairie.
It loves all faces equally
and waits—day after
day—a friend, a brother,
so calm and bland and good.
I never thought till now:
I have no other.

The Saint of Thought

One moment each noon, faced
where the sun is, turn
from events to the church in the stone.
The shade under your hand
welcomes you. Let the lamp
in your forehead explode.

In the long dive of your life
past the sun, these are important,
these meetings. Repeat:
"Rescue me, Day. Hills,
hold the light." Lift your hand.
Let the dark out.

Letting Them Have It

You check out of a big hotel. If the manager
is smart enough, he comes forward
bowing—that's what his life is about.
But if he's dumb he may sit there strangling
himself in the contradictions that existence
piles onto people. The person at the desk
won't realize that the wave of the present has come,
that your birthdays are lined up behind you
like a row of judges looking over your shoulder.
When you walk across the lobby, shifting the world
all the way to Australia, your old friend gravity
follows; you turn at the door and let
everyone in the room have it—their world
back, unaware. They read their newspapers
or look out the windows whistling or just wait
while you carry time away with you, out
wherever you go, lightly, maybe forever.

Craig Volk

Spooky Boots: Go-Go Dancer
For Daniel Lusk & Mark Vinz

Even before the dress
                          you were too bare,
Wasn't the boots,
Was your knees, thighs, arms,
Skull,
All that Dachau tightness
Beneath a hive of hair,
That faceless parade of 90 pounds.

But the dress went,
And shadows etched sharply
As the dance teased and twined,
Each mirror crying: See, See,
This is the black widow.
This is the treacherous web.

And finally to all fours—
A prowling, scattering undulation,

And someone said, "Now that's obscene."

You flipped on your back,
Clawed at the air,

Everything suddenly seemed scarce.

Robert Waldridge

Manifesto

These girls, laughing and chattering,
shattering the rooms with polite smiles.
Who hold filigree and gold,
cold against their muslin breasts
or pressed secretly near the slick bristle of thighs.

Ah! While they sigh in the yellow afternoon,
the sun arches toward Arcturus. . .
flowers bud
like sunrise boiling
from the meadow in my pocket.

These girls, simultaneous
with the revolutionary Spring, with
the anarchist browsing on the tree in my shoulder. . .
They are exhausted bison
shining in the high dying of summer.

And I,
exploding the last words of winter!
dangerous as a moan from dark alleys,
I am caught in the bloody wheat fields,
in love with the hideous Spring.

Marnie Walsh

Bessie Dreaming Bear

we all went to town
one day
went to a store
bought you new shoes
red
high heels
ain't seen you since

John Knew-the-Crow
(1880)

I saw a blue winged bird
sitting silent in the marsh,
his brothers flown away.
Ice grew along his feathers.

I saw a snake
in the forest rock.
She gave me warning.   I gave her none.
I wear hers against my breast.

I saw the buffalo in rut.
They could not see me
for the earth married the sky
and the sound carried off the sun.
I saw the turtle on the grass,
too big, too blind to move.
His neck died beneath my axe
but the claws walked toward the water.

I saw my mother and my father die
and the soldiers took me away.

Cary Waterman

Death On The Farm

Half way between the house and the barn
there is a dead Holstein dairy cow,
black and white like a map of the world.
She is big eared and square toothed,
and frozen solid.

Who ever said death was fluid,
and wore long garments like a wind?
Death is a pile.
The truck from the rendering kitchen
should have been here days ago.
Now it is too late.
The cow is beginning to come back to life.
I can see her breathing from the window.

She looks comfortable there
even though the dogs have begun chewing a dark hole
that will end at the heart.
After they come to take her,
after her fingered milk bag,
her white braced hips are gone
her breathing will go on in that place.
Up and down against the soft weeds,
in and out,
filling with water
the dark space that goes between us
when we are not even looking.

Ramona Weeks

Halloween

Beyond the hopes of friends, the apples sink.
In the cider swimming pool, the sun sits bobbing.
Hallowe'en will come; we'll all go home by midnight:
ghosts escorting girls from Dublin, mice saying
rude things to toads, Bo Peep bandying with a fox.
The black boy with the alarm clock, the hayseed hat,
the battered trumpet, arrives late as candy.

Behind our masks, we are cold creatures.
The jack o'lantern warm without his light is my friend.
A bright tangerine, he dies in morning segments.
Black cats, broomsticks, the whole untidy lot,
return to ordinary corners. Only girls remain,
looking into mirrors, standing backward on the stairs,
searching for shadows; you can see spinsters
tossing apple parings into green leaves
and hoping for passionate initials. A loaf of bread,
loaded with mercury, rides lightly offshore
where the dead man drowned.

The morning after Hallowe'en finds us
almost as we always were. If they wash the hieroglyphic soapings
off our windows, everyone can judge us safe
and move off reassured.

We wait our year out, turning widdershins,
till kirkstones tremble and all time begins backward.
Greensward, swallow our hated rivals; love, like bitumen,
preserve our curses.
What shines, even hate, is sometimes all we know.
Say this, sending me off with ditch water:

"She never begrudged an apple,
saw an enemy she could love,
or helped a drowner who was obsessed with drowning."

Sylvia Wheeler

Earthlings

Just off Santa Fe Trail asphalt,
we are the folks presidents
talk to when times require.

Over the Midwest flyway,
strange birds quack.

Networks make-up women who will not trade
their bleaches, soaps for anything,
to look like us.

After church, we eat fried chicken
with our fingers. T.V. scans
us till bedtime.

Harry lives up the road,
Ike down. Every 40 miles there's a rest stop.
We all say "Howdy." Same inflection.
I can't hardly go on.

James L. White

The Clay Dancer

1

You are buried in so many places
like the scattering of diseased ivory.
The infamous motels of quick nights,
the way you like it and do it best.

The *Morning Star* says you didn't sleep well into spring
and finally gave everything away on blue paper
like the hunter's bow and ashes.

He wakes, touches himself there, looks
at the skin magazine and can't sleep.

2

Toward the last
they said voices summoned you
to write two or three poems a day.
Did you mention the white rooms near Clairmont
or the black roses poised against the stone?
  'No.'

Then what did you write of?
  'The manner of summer suns.
  A walker to spring.
  The false myths of my bloodlines.'

Then what did you write of?
  'How I failed as a man
  or what was asked of my manhood,
  through the long distance,
  dreaming wrong.'

Then what did you write of?
  'Trains under my sleep to Dearborn and beyond.'

Then what did you write of?
  'My first time
  in that hot room.
  The guilt, the shame making it perfect.'

Then what did you write of?
  'Only what I chased.
  Dust in a hundred cities
  and the blind swaying just right.
  Mother hanging sheets by the steaming tub.
  The bluing smell for my father's shirts.
  His white Sunday strolling suit.
  His never being dead enough.'

But did you mention the white rooms near Clairmont
or the black roses by the stone?
  'No, only my first bus to Demming, Texas.'

Then it must be time for you to go.

His heels click against the street as he searches for you.

3

Do you like it this way?
Do you do it often?
Do you like the blind swaying
and the washstand and the cough
in the halls before night?
Do you like the lice-ridden pigeons
cooing their terrible vision of the wino's city?
Do you like the trembling Sunday streets and one cafe?
Do you like my fat body catching breath?
Do you like our sleep filli. · the room?
Can you stay this way a lit. · longer
before your bus to L.A.?

He looks in the dirty movies but you're not there.

4

The cause of death:
These white rooms await the writhing of your life,
well worn and empty.

You enter the echoes
and begin notes on the highway,
the old pickup toward Burntwater
carrying the battered suitcase.

And the poem stops there finally and forever
in the long shadows of the chair
amid the faucets and kitchen smells
where silence is larger than
the room in which you write your life.

It no longer matters that he knows your address.

5

After the last well-saved valium
you do not remember forgiving yourself
in the vomit and urine
but trying to focus on the spreading dahlias
above the bed.

6

The man in leather is finally at your bed.
He strips down to your mother
who wanders through your cold boyhood house
giving out blankets to empty rooms.

A wheel in you forgets to breathe,
and you are dead,
and you know you are dead.

7

Embalmer's report:
He looked like corroded alabaster on the worktable.
His old body, the cracked desert roads, older
than the courthouse square, older than the farmers
spitting their phlegm-filled days,
older than the dirty magazines in the dirty shops
in the dirty cities he so revered.

His open arteries discharged two white colts.
His childless loins repaid
the turquoise, the amber and agate.

His yellowed body finished with the flutes,
finished with the myecins of regret,
finished with the vaporizers and failures,
canceled the bromides and small dreams.
But his eyes wouldn't film
or close, saw further than they should.
Only the two colts remained,
their eyes toward still water,
the blue grass and bean blossom.

8

What goes into heaven with you
so perfectly prepared on the pillow
like a dead satyr?
Lights from the remaining colts
or the cold cafes of November
near your turquoise hands?
The faceless loins?
The rotted coyotes?
The aged owls?
Agate temple?
Corn fire?

None.

You go without streets, songs, or hair.

9

Here at the Del Rio, honey
your shaken steps are voided.
An anonymous patron has picked up your tab.
Your room's off the veranda.
It's quiet here except for weekends
when Reba brings the girls down for the sailors.

You look quite young in your famous blue button-down.
A sax and piano begin the waltz.
Sweet Chocolate sends you your first drink.
The neon lights up tit-pink:
  and the night
  and the night
  and the night!

Ramona Wilson

Visiting Next Door

Her right arm lifts to show the soft dark
hollow   edged by the summer
dress   light as it slides.
She moves her left palm
down the back of his neck
her hips sway very near
his head and shoulders   bare
to the grass cooled air.
She bends and her body begins
a curve
as she leans
to see through the falling light
a small soundless shift
and she could kiss him
in that middle spot where the hair ends
that spot ever like a child's neck.
She cuts the hair of her father
on the new mown lawn.
I think of love at midsummer night.

My dear (as you called me)
            and other adjectives that surely weren't me.
We have waited so long
for time to quit standing still
and speed us up.

My dear (as I sometimes replied)
            being satisified with those names all along
How will you know
when the beat has reached the point
that we can dance with.

All I know is
we have merely bent gently
long enough.

A Fully Grown Woman Goes Berrypicking

Unexpectedly
I come into some huckleberries
sweet   dark
with the coolness of treeshadows
and a faint pine taste
lingering on a dry afternoon
It is so good
to gulp them   bulging mouthfuls
juice exploding
I can't get enough
It was so good then   too
the fire arching the dark out
pines close   black
steaming potatoes   meat hot dripping
eating berries
with those also gone

David Wojahn

Wine
"like cups of wine thrown back into the bottle"
—James Moore

1
Midnight
and the pipes knock.
They call to one another
in their steam language.
George has played his flute
all night in the livingroom,
short pieces, stopping abruptly,
beginning again and again
in search of the right note.
Now he is a child wading into a lake,
learning to swim underwater
in the light the sun brings
to the sand on the lakebed.
I watch him scoop up handfuls of sand
and stone in the blurred green water,
holding them to his face,
just learning to see.

2
Today was the shortest day of the year.
I slept through the afternoon,
walking to lamplight,
to plants watered after sundown.
Outside the neighbors
try to rouse their cars.
Ignitions grind and howl.
The engines complain,
lead aimlessly into the darkness.
I drink wine straight from the bottle
and am already drunk
when my father phones,
talking of the job that's no good,
the money that's not there,
the spine that sways like a willow tree.
He would weep if he could.
"They want to put me in traction,
give me a back brace
for a year and a half."
Who is this stranger who asks me for nothing.

3
I want to talk and
Father, what can I say?
The winter nights are deep red.
We begin to live underwater
in small rooms
filled with flutesong
and the shades pulled down.
We cannot let go of this darkness.
We sit inside it, touch its walls
"like cups of wine thrown back into the bottle."
We write at midnight
with music in the room,
calling our fathers in the black evening,
"regretting nothing."

4
Tonight I am wine.
My father is wine.
The glass sits on the table, full,
with no one to drink it.
This afternoon I dreamt
that my father was running to meet me
and slipped on the ice
into a hole in the lake.
The scene kept repeating itself.
I never reached him in time.
A thick film covered his face
like the eyes of my grandfather,
who died blind, whose last words
were "white, it's white."
Now I swim down
to meet my father in the water,
cupping his face in my hands.
He is crying into my palms
and I can't yet see his face.

Ray A. Young Bear

Four Poems

My reflection
seems upside-down

even when the daylight pushes
my shadow into
the ground

it is like that

_____

this little house swallows
her prayer
through the green fire
and stone

i disappear
into the body of a dog
sleeping over the warm
ashes

_____

i am walking and i
notice that the road
seems bare

some of the stones
are missing

ahead is a toad
throwing stones
from his fingers

whatever thought
he is following
we are following

_____

through the cracks
along the walls of this
house

the sun reaches its peak

our dishes begin
to breathe

Christine Zawadiwsky

My Age Saddens Me

For my birthday I want a burning city
and a weeping willow
and the shadows of all the old men
who live in the hospital
with their battered hats and their swollen arms
and their romping, smiling heart attacks
though I walk among them with my head in the trees,
my hair frozen with spray,
my face bathed in tears. And from my mother I want
a very sharp tongue
to use as a weapon when I join the army, the army
that generals call the world,
and from you I want to hear for the very last time
that you will never see me again.
My brothers and mother, that strong colonade,
promise to protect me
from any tornadoes that might occur before you ask for
reconciliation—that pepper that gives life
a wild, ragged edge though our gingerbread cottage is filled
with screaming children
who know that I'm not your conscience or your mother or
your guardian angel;
and I want a mirror in which your disapproving eyes
will never again be pictured
over my shoulder. Yes for my birthday I want you to return
the last two years
to spend in any way I please, at all costs avoiding
those paper thorns
and that photo of Helen asleep in the gas chamber,
your cat curled near the sill
like a fur-piece or an eel, a bee and its low drone
asleep in his left ear.

Al Zolynas

Two Childhood Memories

I remember my first gun
and my first tangerine.
My father said never
point a gun at a live thing.
I was five and it was my first
gun and besides it was a toy.
I was five and I knew that.
So, I pointed the gun
at my father, at my mother.
It was a big black gun
and it wobbled a lot.
When I pulled the trigger
it went "click,"
and I think my father died.
What I remember about the tangerine
is how easily the skin came off.

Experiences The Ancients Never Had:
The Instant Replay

We can have it again
and again—speeded up, slowed down, stopped
at the crucial point:
the knock-out punch,
the rare triple play, the race-car
exploding against the wall,
the suicide stepping off the ledge.
We can play it again and again Sam
to our heart's horrible content.
We can even have it reversed:
the diver sucked feet first out of the water,
landing on the board perfectly dry.
At night we dream
with the help of camera techniques:
jump-cuts, fade-outs, slow-mo.
The same old dreams: the snake pits,
the flying over vast cities,
the appointment we have with someone
somewhere, but have never kept yet.

Appendix: Authors and Poems by Issue

Dacotah Territory 1
Robert Bly, "Driving Toward Dacotah Territory"
Gene Frumkin, "Long and Shadowy Habits"
Richard Lyons, "Chicago"
Thomas McGrath, "Giuffre's Nightmusic" and "In Early Autumn"
Marnie Walsh, "Bessie Dreaming Bear"

Dacotah Territory 2
Alvaro Cardona-Hine, "Two Poems from the Garden" and "Christmas Eve"
David Ignatow, "It's snowing..." and "The trees..."
William Stafford, "Waking in the Midwest"
Marnie Walsh, "John Knew-the-Crow"

Dacotah Territory 3
Robert Bly, "Thinking of Seclusion"
Roland Flint, "Prayer, Poor Sinners, Homely Girls"
Don Gordon, "Memorial Day"
W.S. Merwin, "To the Hand"
John Calvin Rezmerski, "Tarzan" and "Manifesto"
Gary Snyder, "Manzanita"

Dacotah Territory 4
B. Doyle, "The Diving Horse Act"
Stephen Dunn, "Palominos" (originally titled "Real Toads")
Alvin Greenberg, "The House of the Would-Be Gardener: VI"
Joseph Hopkins, "Writer, Sunday: San Francisco"
Antony Oldknow, "Baptism in Kansas"

Dacotah Territory 5
Robert Bly, "Late Moon"
James Fawbush, "Driving Home from Park River, North Dakota in August" (reprinted in **DT** 11)
Patricia Hampl, "The Marsh at Boy River, Minnesota"
Rory Holscher, "Mississippi Valley Slowdown"
Richard Hugo, "Living Alone" and "Places and Ways to Live"
Dale Jacobson, "Our Hands" and "The Child Running Toward His Death"
William Stafford, "A Local Statement"

Dacotah Territory 6
Joy Harjo, "Going Toward Pojoaque, A December Full Moon / 72" and "Kansas City Coyote"
Roberta Hill, "E Uni Que A The A Tho, Father"
Simon Ortiz, "The Creation: According to Coyote"
Ramona Wilson, "A Fully Grown Woman Goes Berry Picking" and "Visiting Next Door"

Dacotah Territory 7
Gene Frumkin, "Passing By"
John Judson, "Master Charge"
Miriam Levine, "Working: The Egg Keeper"
Howard Mohr, "Ralph Nader Visits My House"
Joe Paddock, "Eating Wild Food"
Mary Pryor, "Weasel"
William Stafford, "The Saint of Thought"

Dacotah Territory 8/9
Noreen Ayres, "Turncoat"
Franklin Brainard, "The Edge of Boundaries"
Michael Dennis Browne, "Bad Poems," (reprinted in **DT** 11)
Art Cuelho, "A Drifter's Brand"
William D. Elliott, "By the Sea, I Speak of Winter"
Carol Frost, "A Small Bird, Kept"
Alvin Greenberg, "The Sealed Room Mystery"
Joseph Hopkins, "How I Won at the Olympic Games"
Stanley Kiesel, "Lines On No One"
John Knoepfle, "why are you here..." and "spoiled meat and starvation..."
Ted Kooser, "Shooting A Farmhouse"
Richard Lyons, "Restricted Love" and "The Fan Dancer"
Thomas McGrath, "Totems (V)" and "From A Long Way from Pah-Gotzin-Kay"
William Meissner, "Salvage" and "Colors"
David Solheim, "Containers" and "Breaking Up"

Dacotah Territory 10
Marisha Chamberlain, "The Stars Are Apple Clusters"
Philip Dacey, "Bedtime Song"
Margaret Hasse, "My Mother's Lullaby" (reprinted in **DT** 11)
Robert Hedin, "Houdini"
Ruth Roston, "Children's Theatre"
Sylvia Wheeler, "Earthlings"

Dacotah Territory 11
Jenne'Andrews, "Turning with the Ears of the Horse"
Kate Basham, "At A Retrospective of Chinese Art"
Michael Dennis Browne, "Captain Cat"
David Martinson, "In Praise of Neglected Ladders"
James Moore, "Death-House"
John Calvin Rezmerski, "Your Hands"
Cary Waterman, "Death on the Farm"

Dacotah Territory 12
Dave Etter, "Bright Mississippi" and "Postcard to Florida"
Carolyn Forche, "Mientras Dure Vida, Sobra El Tiempo"
Ray A. Young Bear, "Four Poems"
Al Zolynas, "Two Childhood Memories" and "Experiences the Ancients Never Had:
        The Instant Replay"

Dacotah Territory 13
Carl Cunningham, "Ropes from Sky"
Stephen Dunn, "South Jersey Pastoral"
Roland Flint, "At 4 A.M. in the Kitchen" and "Starting A Notebook at New Year's"
Gene Frumkin, "The Moon at Canyon de Chelly"
Don Gordon, "Mortal"
Kate Green, "Letter to My Life"
Richard Grossman, "Frog," "Porcupine" and "Viper" (originally entitled "Snake")
Dan Jaffe, "I Have No Way with Gardens" and "For Langston Hughes"
William Kloefkorn, "Haywire Cox" and "Some Day This Will Happen to Us Too"
Craig Volk, "Spooky Boots: Go-Go Dancer"
Robert Waldridge, "Manifesto"
Ramona Weeks, "Halloween"

Dacotah Territory 14
William Burns, "Alcoholic: The Morning Beckon"
D.W. Donzella, "Those Spring Girls"
Patricia Goedicke, "In the Body Shop"
Ralph J. Mills, Jr., "The Moon" and "Across the Cold"
Christine Zawadiwsky, "My Age Saddens Me"

Dacotah Territory 15
Constance Egemo, "The Keeper"
Alvin Greenberg, "The Arts of the Midwest"
Joanne Hart, "When Your Parents Grow Old"
Rory Holscher, "A Beatitude"
Ted Kooser, "Walking to Work"
Richard Lyons, "Of Robert Lowell"
Robert Schuler, "Old Testament"
David Wojahn, "Wine"

Dacotah Territory 16
Joseph Duemer, "The Burning of the Ozark Hotel"
Ted Kooser, "A Hairnet with Stars"
Daniel Lusk, "Understudy"
William Stafford, "Letting Them Have It"
James L. White, "The Clay Dancer"

Dacotah Territory 17
John Caddy, "Sharing the Cry"
Dan Jaffe, "Poem for A Bar Mitzva"
Deborah Keenan, "A Poem About White Flowers"
Michael Moos, "The Archer"
David Ray, "The Father of the Curious Child"
George Roberts, "Thanking My Father for Reading to Me"
Paul Shuttleworth, "Mow"

Acknowledgements

In lieu of contributor notes, we have decided to list the books in which many of these poems were eventually reprinted, or, in some cases simply the most recent book of the author. We gratefully acknowledge all permissions for reprinting.

To the best of our knowledge, **Dacotah Territory** retains copyright privileges on the poems in this collection by B. Doyle, D.W. Donzella, Joseph Duemer, Roberta Hill, Rory Holscher, and Christine Zawadiwsky. By the time of printing we were unable to establish contact with these authors, but we felt strongly that their poems should nonetheless be included in the collection.

All rights to material published in this book belong to the individual authors and publishers, and any reproduction or reprinting of this material may be done only with their permission.

Jenné Andrews, *In Pursuit of the Family* (Minnesota Writers Publishing House)
Robert Bly, *This Tree Will Be Here for A Thousand Years* (Harper & Row)
Franklin Brainard, *36 Poems, A Memorial Edition* (Uzzano Press)
Michael Dennis Brown, *The Sun-Fetcher* (Carnegie-Mellon University Press)
William Burns, *Dark Leverage* (Trunk Press)
Alvaro Cardona-Hine, *The Half-Eaten Angel* (Nodin Press)
Art Cuelho, *The Last Foot of Shade* (Holmgangers Press)
Philip Dacey, *The Boy Under the Bed* (John Hopkins University Press)
Joseph Duemer, *Fool's Paradise* (Charles Street Press)
Stephen Dunn, *Looking for Holes in the Ceiling* (University of Massachusetts Press), *Work And Love*
   (Carnegie-Mellon University Press)
Dave Etter, *Central Standard Time* (Bk Mk Press), *Bright Mississippi* (Juniper Press),
   Alliance, Illinois (Kylix Press)
James Fawbush, *Great Grandpa Nettestad Was Blind* (Territorial Press)
Roland Flint, *And Morning* and *Say It* (Dryad Press)
Carolyn Forché, *Gathering the Tribes* (Yale University Press)
Carol Frost, *The Salt Lesson* (Graywolf Press)
Gene Frumkin, *Clouds and Red Earth* (Swallow / Ohio University Press)
Patricia Goedicke, *The Trail That Turns on Itself* (Ithaca House)
Don Gordon, *On the Ward* and *Excavations* (West Coast Poetry Review)
Kate Green, *The Bell in the Silent Body* (Minnesota Writers Publishing House)
Alvin Greenberg, *The House of the Would-Be Gardener* (New Rivers Press),
   Metaform (University of Massachusetts Press)
Richard Grossman, *The Animals* (Zygote Press)
Patricia Hampl, *Woman Before An Aquarium* (University of Pittsburgh Press)
Joy Harjo, *What Moon Drove Me to This* (I. Reed Books)
Robert Hedin, *Snow Country* and *At the Home-Altar* (Copper Canyon Press)
Richard Hugo, *Selected Poems*, and *What Thou Lovest Well Remains American*
   (poems reprinted by permission of the author and publisher,
     W.W. Norton & Company, Inc. ©1975)
Roberta Hill, See *Carriers of the Dream Wheel: Contemporary Native American Poetry*, ed.
   Duane Niatum (Harper & Row)
David Ignatow, *Facing the Tree* (Atlantic Monthly Press) and *Whisper to the Earth*
   (forthcoming, Atlantic / Little Brown)
Dale Jacobson, *Poems for Goya's Disparates* (Jazz Press)
Dan Jaffe, *Dan Freeman* (University of Nebraska Press)
John Judson, *North of Athens* (Spoon River Press)
Deborah Keenan, *Household Wounds* (New Rivers Press)
Stanley Kiesel, *The Pearl Is A Hardened Sinner* (Nodin Press)
William Kloefkorn, *Not Such A Bad Place to Be* (Copper Canyon Press)
John Knoepfle, *Poems for the Hours* (Uzzano Press)
Ted Kooser, *Sure Signs* (University of Pittsburgh Press)
Miriam Levine, *Friends Dreaming* (Ironwood Press)
Richard Lyons, *Scanning the Land* (North Dakota Institute for Regional Studies)
David Martinson, *Bleeding the Radiator* (Territorial Press)
Thomas McGrath, *The Movie at the End of the World* (Swallow Press), *Waiting for the Angel*
   (Uzzano Press)
William Meissner, *Learning to Breathe Under Water* (Ohio University Press)
W.S. Merwin, *Unframed Originals* and *Writings to An Unfinished Accompaniment* (Atheneum)

Ralph J. Mills, Jr., *Living with Distance* (BOA Editions) and *Night Roads* (The Rook Press)
Howard Mohr, *How to Tell A Tornado* (Prairie Home Companion)
James Moore, *The New Body* (University of Pittsburgh Press)
Michael Moos, *Hawk Hover* (Territorial Press)
Antony Oldknow, *Consolation for Beggars* (Song Press)
Simon Ortiz, *From Sand Creek* (Thunder's Mouth Press), *Going for Rain* (Harper & Row)
Mary Pryor, *The Bicycle in the Snowbank* (Territorial Press)
David Ray, *Tramp's Cup* (Chariton Review Press)
John Calvin Rezmerski, *An American Gallery* (Three Rivers Press)
George Roberts, *Night Visits to A Wolf's Howl* (Oyster Press)
Ruth Roston, *I Live in the Watchmaker's Town* (New Rivers Press)
Robert Schuler, *Where Is Dancer's Hill?* (Lame Johnny Press), *Red Cedar Scroll*
          (Crow King Editions)
Paul Shuttleworth, *Always Autumn* (Nebraska Review Chapbooks)
Gary Snyder, *Turtle Island* (New Directions)
David Solheim, *On the Ward* (Territorial Press)
William Stafford, *Stories That Could Be True, New and Collected Poems* (Harper & Row).
          Things That Happen Where There Aren't Any People (BOA Editions)
Craig Volk, *Icarus Above the Prairie* (Pierian Press)
Robert Waldridge, *From A Place Which Is No Longer Named* (Territorial Press)
Marnie Walsh, *A Taste of the Knife* (Ahsahta Press)
Cary Waterman, *The Salamander Migration and Other Poems* (reprinted by permission of the
          University of Pittsburgh Press, ©1980 by Cary Waterman)
Sylvia Wheeler, *This Can't Go On Forever* (Raindust Press)
James L. White, *The Salt Ecstasies* (Graywolf Press), *The Del Rio Hotel* (Territorial Press)
David Wojahn, *Icehouse Lights* (Yale University Press)
Ray A. Young Bear, *The Winter of the Salamander* (Harper & Row)
Christine Zawadiwsky, *Sleeping with the Enemy* (Floating Island Publications)
Al Zolynas, *The New Physics* (Wesleyan University Press)

DACOTAH
TERRITORY